PENGUIN ANANDA

FROM CHAOS TO CALM

Gauranga Darshan Das, a disciple of His Holiness Radhanath Swami, is a distinguished educator and bestselling spiritual author of over thirty-five books. He holds a master's degree in systems science and automation from the prestigious Indian Institute of Science, Bengaluru. During his brief corporate career, spanning approximately two years, he conducted research at esteemed organizations such as TCS Innovation Labs, resulting in the publication of over ten technical papers and filing of a provisional patent. His unique journey also led him to embrace the path of monkhood in 2009.

In his current role as the dean of Bhaktivedanta Vidyapitha at ISKCON Govardhan Ecovillage, outside Mumbai, Gauranga Darshan Das conducts spiritual education programmes on both residential and online platforms. He is a prolific speaker and teacher, renowned for presenting timeless wisdom in a lucid and contemporary form to diverse audiences, including children, teens, professionals and educators. He travels to places around India, Australia, the United States, etc., to share wisdom in various forums, including temples, ashrams, schools, colleges and the corporate sector. He has lectured for over 7500 hours and conducted more than fifty online courses (www.vidyapitha.in).

As an accomplished author, Gauranga Darshan Das has penned several study guides (the Subodhini series), storybooks, self-enrichment works (*Dhruva*, *Disapproved but Not Disowned* and *Answers to Life's Questions*, among others) and children's literature (Mindful Me, Bhagavatam Tales and Gita Wisdom Tales series). He runs a monthly ezine called *Bhagavata Pradipika* whilst penning thought-inspiring articles for international and Indian *Back to Godhead* magazines. His dedication to the dissemination of spiritual wisdom has made him a respected figure in spiritual, educational and corporate circles.

Know more about him on www.gaurangadarshan.com.

ADVANCE PRAISE FOR THE BOOK

'The Bhagavad-Gita has inspired generations of thinkers, seekers and intrepid life-explorers. The Sanskrit verses answer the questions deep within our hearts and address the most fundamental human dilemmas. Yet, we require learned individuals who live and breathe the text to bring out that beauty. For this we thank Gauranga Darshan Das. He has ingeniously extracted pertinent life lessons that [will] empower us to navigate the modern battlefield of the urban jungle with grace and resilience. This book won't let you down; rather, you may find you can't put it down'—S.B. Keshava Swami, spiritual author and community mentor

'The timeless beauty of the Gita lies in its enduring lessons, taught by the Lord to the young Arjuna, the world's greatest archer, on the battlefield thousands of years ago. These teachings remain as pertinent today as they were then. Gauranga Darshan Das, with his profound understanding of our scriptures, stands out as an exceptional speaker, teacher and spiritual author. In *From Chaos to Calm*, he brilliantly encapsulates the essence of the Gita, making its wisdom relevant to contemporary life. This serves as a powerful reminder that peace and clarity are attainable, even in today's complex world'—Ajay Piramal, chairman, Piramal Group

'This book offers apt and subtle transformative guidance with balanced doses of a maturity-enhancing elixir. This enriching treatise is a must-read for all, young and old. Every reader is bound to develop themselves with a sense of calm and serenity, thus enhancing their level of wisdom'—Shriya Saran, actor and Kathak dancer

'As a soldier who has faced the extremes of war, I have come to deeply appreciate the value of inner peace. In *From Chaos to Calm*, Gauranga Darshan Das draws timeless lessons from the Bhagavad-Gita and presents them in a way that resonates with modern life. His wisdom offers practical guidance for finding serenity amidst the chaos of today's world. This book is an essential read for anyone looking to transform their life's challenges into opportunities for personal growth and calm'—Yogendra Singh Yadav, Param Vir Chakra, Kargil War

'Transformative and profound, *From Chaos to Calm* distils the timeless teachings of the Gita into practical insights, addressing contemporary life's challenges with clarity and compassion. This book is a guiding light, leading us towards inner peace and balance'—Shubha Vilas, author, educationalist and leadership consultant

ALSO BY THE SAME AUTHOR

Study Guides

Gītā Subodhinī
Īśopanishad Subodhinī
Upadeśāmrta Subodhinī
Bhakti Rasāmṛta Subodhinī
Caitanya Subodhinī (4 volumes)
Bhāgavata Subodhinī (10 volumes)
The Art of Studying & Teaching Scriptures

Self-Enrichment

Dhruva
Secrets of Bhakti
Caitanya Pravāha
Bhāgavata Pravāha
Answers to Life's Questions
Disapproved but Not Disowned

Illustrated Children's Books

Mindful Me
Bhāgavatam Tales (6 volumes)
Gita Wisdom Tales (5 volumes)
Ramayana to Inspire Young Minds

Shloka Books (Pocket Size)

Gītā Ratnamālā
Gītā Tattvamālā
Caitanya Ratnamālā
Bhāgavata Tattvamālā
Bhāgavata Ratnamālā (2 volumes)

FROM CHAOS TO CALM

108 PRACTICES FROM THE GITA FOR INNER BALANCE

GAURANGA DARSHAN DAS

PENGUIN
ANANDA
An imprint of Penguin Random House

PENGUIN ANANDA

Penguin Ananda is an imprint of the Penguin Random House group of companies
whose addresses can be found at global.penguinrandomhouse.com

Published by Penguin Random House India Pvt. Ltd
4th Floor, Capital Tower 1, MG Road,
Gurugram 122 002, Haryana, India

Penguin
Random House
India

First published in Penguin Ananda by Penguin Random House India 2024

10 9 8 7 6 5 4 3 2 1

ISBN 9780143463610

Typeset in Cardo by MAP Systems, Bengaluru, India

www.penguin.co.in

Contents

Author's Note

Of the many spiritual texts I have perused so far, I found something unique about the Bhagavad-Gita. It is a divine discussion that took place within the context of a deadly battle. A renowned bowman renounces his bow on the chariot, and the Lord, acting as the charioteer, begins to sing.

In the layers of the Gita, I found engaging questions that could bridge the gap between theory and practice, solutions that could percolate into the marrow of your daily life and help you transcend its challenges. Thus, I found reason to come up with *From Chaos to Calm*—a plethora of lively discussions that resonates with the pulse of modern-day dilemmas.

Is there such a thing as justifiable anger? What truly distinguishes love from lust? Why do I seem to be the beloved of pain? Does God play favourites? These questions, and the transformative journey to find their answers, became the heartbeat of my exploration—a journey deeply rooted in the wisdom of the Gita.

Today, as you hold this book in your hands, it's essential to understand that this isn't just paper and ink. Instead, it is a vibrant tapestry of lively discussions—an invitation to engage in conversations that tackle real-life problems. Within these discussions, you won't find abstract theories that remain aloof from your daily struggles. Instead, you'll discover actionable practices that resonate with the challenges you face, providing a pathway to rise above them.

From Chaos to Calm serves as an unconventional guide, offering you a unique opportunity to engage in a dialogue that intricately dissects the complexities of existence. Rather than simply presenting wisdom, it invites you to participate in a dynamic conversation that encourages questioning, seeking solutions and ultimately adopting practices that infuse vitality into your personal journey. Moreover, I have infused in it personal experiences, analogies and anecdotes that I pray will enhance your reading experience and inspire practical application.

Welcome to *From Chaos to Calm*, a profound exploration of the Gita, where vibrant, pulsating discussions abound, promising to reshape your life into something greater than it was yesterday.

1

Blossoming into Uniqueness

Redefining Success on Your Own Terms

One day, I was invited to address an assembly of about 3000 students and teachers, on the occasion of Teachers' Day. My talk was about an hour long, where I spoke primarily based on the Bhagavad-Gita, along with examples from the Mahabharata, Ramayana and Bhagavata Purana. The topic I had to speak on was the teacher–student relationship.

Somewhere in the middle of the discussion, I asked the students, 'What if you score 95 per cent in your test, will you be happy?'

There were smiles while some of the kids replied, 'Yes! Yes! Of course, that's a great score.'

I followed up with another question. 'What if you're the only person who got 95 per cent, and all your classmates scored higher, like 96, 97, 98? Would you still be happy?'

The excitement seemed to abate; after all, that would mean scoring 95 per cent but still lagging far behind the others.

I shot another question. 'What if you get 60 per cent in your math exam? Would you be happy?'

There was quite a rattling silence.

Then, I made a second comment. 'What if all your classmates got 50 per cent, 40 per cent and less than that?'

'Yes, we will be happy,' most of the kids replied. After all, scoring 60 per cent meant becoming the topper.

I continued, 'Oftentimes, we feel happy or sad about our performance depending on how others perform. Consciously or unconsciously, our feelings are often influenced by comparison or competition with people around us. Many a time, even the world expects us to produce attention-attracting results, and we tend to feel successful only when we could produce results that impress them.'

Sometimes, people see the nature of results we produce, more than the sincere effort we put in.

Then I concluded saying, 'If you had scored 60 per cent in your previous test, and 70 per cent now, that should make you happy, because there is an improvement in your performance. Be happy irrespective of how much others score, and where you stand in comparison with their performance. Compete with yourself, not with others. Focus on self-growth, and not on defeating people around you.'

Prioritize self-improvement over outsmarting others.

Shifting our focus from proving ourselves to improving ourselves relieves us from the pain of comparison and burden of competition.

The Motivation behind Learning

Arjuna was the favourite student of his military teacher, Drona. Arjuna sincerely put his efforts into mastering the art of archery, but his motivation was to learn the arts as a part of his *kshatriya* responsibility and utilize that skill to protect righteousness and innocent people. It was the responsibility of the princes of the royal order to fight miscreants and defend those who follow virtue in the kingdom.

In contrast, there was another warrior in the Mahabharata named Karna who learnt archery not exactly to protect *dharma* and the innocent citizens but to outsmart Arjuna. He had an ambition to be known, recognized and praised as the best archer in the world. For that, he even lied to Lord Parasurama so he could learn military science.

Obsession makes one lose discretion.

Arjuna found satisfaction, happiness and contentment in utilizing his military art for good deeds, directly under the guidance of the Almighty Lord Krishna. But Karna was always burning with a desire to outdo Arjuna. Karna aligned himself with Duryodhana, who was well known as an evil person. Duryodhana supported Karna, seeing his expertise in archery which he thought could be used against the Pandavas in the future. Karna, in turn, exhibited loyalty for the motivated favour he received.

Coming back to the point of 'satisfaction in learning' versus 'the kick of outsmarting others', the latter always

proves to be futile and frustrating. One should aspire for absolute happiness found in one's sincere intentions and actions, rather than the relative happiness derived from defeating others.

Be on a quest for personal growth, and not in a race to defeat others.

Being Yourself

Everybody is gifted in a unique way, and intelligent people utilize their natural talents and skills for good deeds. While the chaotic situation of the world constantly induces us to compare ourselves with others, compete with them, defeat them, imitate them and so on, the Gita advises to stick to our particular duties instead of imitating others. Lord Krishna says in the Bhagavad-Gita (3.35),

śreyān sva-dharmo viguṇah
para-dharmāt sv-anuṣṭhitāt
sva-dharme nidhanam śreyah
para-dharmo bhayāvahah

'It is better to perform one's own duties even with some shortcomings, than performing another's duties perfectly. Imitating others or taking up someone else's duties leads to unnecessary anxiety.'

This verse emphasizes the importance of being oneself, instead of trying to be like someone else. Dress, hairstyle, shoes or any fashion that fits one person may

not suit everyone. Similarly, a person may excel at an activity, but not everyone may have a flair for doing so. Lord Shiva drank poison to protect the people in the universe and that poison created a blue mark on his neck, which is considered to be his ornament. If people try imitating Lord Shiva and drink poison, what do you think will happen to them?

> *What one person can do, others need not do, sometimes cannot do, and sometimes should not do, at least not by compromising on what they are meant to do.*

In the Gita, Arjuna is seen expressing his desire to live a life of begging instead of fighting with his own relatives for a prosperous kingdom. Begging is traditionally associated with *brahmanas* or ascetics, but a *kshatriya* ruler's duty is to rule, administer justice and protect the innocent. Although Arjuna desired a life of begging, Lord Krishna advised him not to adopt the activities of a *brahmana* but do his duty as a *kshatriya*.

When you go to an apparel store, you may find a dress that is advertised as the best, but it's up to you to understand whether it is truly the best for *you*. Often, due to the propaganda of this world, we adopt certain behaviours, styles, trends or career options, seeing their popularity and attractive traits. Just because a social influencer garners the attention of millions on social media, that does not mean everybody should become a YouTuber, social media influencer or a life coach. Just because someone acts well on the screen and gains a good

fan following, it does not mean someone who is not good at it should imitate them at the cost of losing other promising career options.

In life, we have to choose not what is best, but what is best for us.

Once, I heard an example that convinced me of the importance of being true to one's nature: 'A monkey can never win a swimming competition against a fish. And a fish can never win a tree-climbing competition against a monkey.' So, unnecessary comparisons and competition must be avoided by all means.

Unhealthy comparisons and unrealistic aspirations and endeavours can spoil one's organic course of life.

Sculptors diligently carve out statues from materials like stone, metals like gold, silver and brass, or wood, clay or plaster. Although stunning statues can be made out of all these materials, the effort required to carve out a statue depends on the material's characteristics and flexibility. Some materials are easy to work upon, and some take more effort and time. Nevertheless, the sculptor's aim is to manifest a beautiful statue from the particular materials they are working on.

All of us are sculptors of our own lives. Although every individual ultimately seeks the (statue of) satisfaction in life, some derive it through one particular field or occupation while others through other occupations. Everybody's journey is unique. So, let's not be disappointed or feel

jealous that others are effortlessly accomplishing things while we are struggling to attain the same.

Celebrate Your Uniqueness

The look and feel of a wooden statue and a stone statue are different, although they are of the same size and shape, but their sculptors are happy to see the final product and experience satisfaction in their sincere efforts. And those who look at the statues appreciate them for their unique features and the diligent effort put in to manifest them. Similarly, the performance and productivity of different individuals are of different natures, but as long as the effort is sincere and the process is honest, they can be satisfied at heart. Therefore, let's work with integrity, celebrate our uniqueness and open up to the diversity around us without jealousy or insecurity.

If one is genuinely interested in a particular field, one can take inspiration from role models in those fields, diligently learn the art, eventually gain experience and mastery, and excel in those fields. This is called organic growth. However, persistently pursuing an area despite continued failures, especially at the cost of losing valuable time, and giving up natural opportunities to excel in one's suitable field may not be wise. Being attracted to a certain field is fine, but if it's primarily due to the public attention it gets and not the compatibility that we have with it, then it is definitely not sustainable.

Sculptors mould the material they are handling with diligent effort but they cannot modify its characteristics.

Stone and wood are different materials and can never substitute each other in look and feel. Similarly, we can refine our talents with diligent effort, but we must have the humility to accept our limitations as well. Let's utilize whatever God-given talents and resources we have to excel in life, although our achievements may not match others'. The Gita's wisdom echoes in the importance of humility and sincerity, to stick to our particular work instead of imitating others or comparing and competing with them. What might be a cakewalk for one person could pose great difficulty for another.

A harmonious approach to a fulfilling life includes this trio:

1. Sincerity to accept what can't be changed
2. Diligence to improve wherever one can
3. Wisdom to discern between the two

Just as sculptors recognize the distinct characteristics of each material, as individuals we should acknowledge our own strengths and limitations.

Moreover, the different roles in this world, be it an athlete, singer, doctor, writer, engineer or architect, contribute to a vibrant society with variety and without monotony. We all are like unique puzzle pieces. We don't have to change who we are to fit in. Each puzzle piece is special. Our friends are like other puzzle pieces, and they should fit with us naturally.

Derive satisfaction in being the best version of yourself without the burden of comparison and longing for public attention.

Seek Satisfaction, not Attention!

Public attention is not a reliable parameter to assess satisfaction levels. One who is always in the limelight with millions of eyes on them may not be satisfied at heart, and it could be a great discomfort for them to stand amidst the public, giving autographs and taking selfies. On the other hand, someone may be genuinely satisfied at heart despite minimal public attention, with a few loving friends and family members, and a consistent source of livelihood, absorption and spiritual practices.

Once, my beloved guru, Radhanath Swami, said, 'I do so many things to feel a sense of satisfaction.' Pointing out to a mother in front of him with a little baby on her lap, he continued, 'But when I see this mother feeling so happy just by seeing her baby smile, I think her happiness is much greater than mine.'

The real satisfaction is in doing what you can do naturally, and not in what you are induced to do by popular opinion and for public attention.

There is nothing wrong with being ambitious, but if that ambition does not lead to the satisfaction of the heart, there is something inherently wrong with that kind of ambition.

Let's look for satisfaction in our efforts, and not in recognition for them.

Don't deprive yourself of the satisfaction in personal growth, by being disappointed for not getting the attention you expected.

Societal Expectations

Sometimes, being unable to fulfil others' expectations can also demotivate us so much that we might become dysfunctional. Not that we shouldn't try to please others, but we shouldn't lose track of what truly matters to us while conforming ourselves to societal expectations.

Unfortunately, many of our peers, and sometimes even parents and society have certain stereotyped expectations from us. They are impressed only when we are in the limelight. Consciously or unconsciously, we think, work and aim to fulfil their expectations. We may think we are successful only when others are impressed with our achievements. And we want to be the toppers, go-getters, achievers, accomplishers, leaders, performers and so on!

Does it mean that those who are not in the limelight are useless? Are they not entitled to satisfaction or the joys of life?

If happiness lies only in big achievements and attention-grabbing results, then hardly 0.1 per cent of the world's population would be entitled to happiness. What about the other 99.9 per cent?

> *Real happiness is not in astonishing or outsmarting others, but in self-improvement.*

We need not compete with others, but we can surely compete with ourselves. Taking inspiration from others who are doing better than us, instead of trying to compete with them, can help us get on this path of organic competition.

When we seek pleasure in winning a competition with others, we are aspiring for a relative happiness. When we seek to improve ourselves, we are aspiring for absolute happiness.

Succumbing to peer pressure or undue societal expectations is totally unnecessary. Instead of competing with others, focusing on our own growth and progress would help us remain functional and mobile under all circumstances. Everybody has a unique ability to understand and accomplish things. Let's learn to embrace our uniqueness and celebrate the little victories, knowing that each step forward is a triumph in our own story. What is good for us need not be good for others. What is good for others need not be the best for us.

We're not in a race to be better than others; we're on a quest to become the best version of ourselves.

Inspiration vs Jealousy

Sometimes, successful people may become our beacon of inspiration. Their progress may make us think, 'Wow, I want to get better like them!' This will help us grow and resultantly give our best.

On the flip side, if we think, 'Oh no, they're better than me,' or 'I'm better than them,' that can allow feelings like jealousy or pride to creep into our hearts. Such comparisons associated with unhealthy emotions can stress out our mind and may also leave our friendships strained.

Focus on being the best version of yourself instead of thinking about who's better or worse than you.

Unhealthy comparisons can lead to inferiority and superiority complexes.

Inferiority Complex and Envy

An inferiority complex is a mental condition where we consistently feel inadequate, inherently flawed, unworthy or less competent than others. It results from unhealthy comparisons, unrealistic standards, past experiences or societal expectations.

Those who suffer from an inferiority complex develop envy towards those they perceive as more successful, competent or accomplished. Envy indicates a strong desire to possess qualities or achievements that others have, leading to feelings of resentment or frustration. An inferiority complex or envy can significantly impact our emotional and psychological well-being.

Superiority Complex and Pride

A superiority complex is characterized by an exaggerated belief in one's own abilities, status or accomplishments, in comparison to others. Such people tend to overestimate their own importance, competence or intelligence while underestimating others.

Having a healthy sense of satisfaction in one's own achievements or qualities, and not looking down upon

others, is all right. However, when such self-belief becomes excessive and evolves into an attitude of superiority, one become proud, arrogant and overconfident.

Those who suffer from a superiority complex lack empathy and tend to stay aloof from others. It strains relationships.

Instead of constantly comparing ourselves with others and experiencing a superiority complex or inferiority complex, we can learn to shift our focus to upgrading ourselves.

Rising above Unhealthy Competitive Spirit

Staying true to ourselves empowers us to make choices aligned with our own values and interests rather than succumbing to external pressures.

Sometimes, when we see someone achieving something more significant, we may experience our joy being stolen. Therefore, giving up the habit of comparing ourselves with others is essential for discovering the happiness we genuinely deserve.

Instead of envying someone who outperformed us, we can try to appreciate them for their good qualities and achievements. Instead of feeling puffed up about our achievements, we can try to honestly thank all those who have supported and helped us in our endeavour. Thus, we can happily celebrate our success without looking down upon any one. This is the key to mitigating a superiority complex and pride, and it is also the door to good friendships.

We can also try writing down our thoughts, feelings and achievements to create a personal record of our journey. Reflecting on our experiences can shift the focus from external comparisons to internal growth.

Social media often promotes unrealistic standards and fosters unhealthy comparison or competition. I suggest it would be prudent to limit our time on social media platforms and be mindful of how they can impact our self-perception. We could possibly use the time we save to interact with 'real' people.

Thus, using these techniques, we can live a blissful life free from the disease of comparison!

One who constantly compares oneself with others also tends to compete with others. An unhealthy competitive spirit and constant attempts to outsmart and defeat others create stress. But now, at this point, the secret to dusting off such stress is yours!

Practices for Inner Balance

1. *Prioritize Personal Growth:* Shift your focus from proving yourself to improving yourself. Celebrate achievements that represent growth, even if they don't surpass others. Rise above comparison and competition.
2. *Embrace Your Uniqueness:* Be authentic and true to yourself. Aim for goals that align with your values and resonate with your individual strengths, talents and interests, and avoid imitating others.
3. *Seek Intrinsic Satisfaction:* Strive for personal satisfaction in your efforts rather than seeking external validation. Satisfaction derived from genuine efforts is more fulfilling than attention garnered for the sake of popularity.
4. *Inspiration over Jealousy:* Look up to successful people as inspiration rather than fostering jealousy. Focus on being the best version of yourself instead of comparing your success to others.
5. *Cultivate Healthy Perspectives:* Avoid detrimental comparisons that lead to inferiority or superiority complexes. Understand that everyone's journey is unique, and success is subjective and multifaceted.
6. *Limit Social Media Exposure:* Be mindful of the impact of social media on your self-perception. Limit your time on social media platforms and engage more with real people as these interactions foster genuine connections.

2

Journey to Inner Strength

Mastering Tolerance in Life's Dualities

It was in June 2009 that I decided to take to monkhood along with a close-knit group of youngsters, primarily in our early twenties. The first year was meant for an immersive training experience. Our training destination was the serene Govardhan Ecovillage, located about 100 km from Mumbai. This peaceful and picturesque farm community provided the perfect backdrop for our training, during which we delved into the profound teachings of the Bhagavad-Gita under the guidance of a revered senior monk.

Our daily routine unfolded with morning prayers, Gita teachings, nature strolls and lighthearted conversations. We had nourishing meals, mostly self-cooked, but we also had the chance of feasting on some big chapattis lovingly made by the elderly village ladies. As the sun dipped below the horizon, another senior monk would read to us the

sweet childhood stories of Lord Krishna. Listening to them, we would welcome slumber in the silence of the night at the Ecovillage, far, far away from the hubbub and blaring horns of the city roads.

Those days, we were short on electricity, and the Internet was almost a luxury. None of us had smartphones, and some didn't have a phone at all. Phone or no phone—the network coverage always appeared to be playing a game of hide-and-seek all through this countryside set-up. But we had each other, and some sweet friendly interactions in a rustic ambience, with the Bhagavad-Gita in our laps and its verses on our tongues. A part of our training was to learn the Gita *shlokas*, and I admit, it was thrilling. We would keep singing out these *mantras* while on walks, before and after eating, and even while bathing. In fact, the concepts of the Gita were the crux of almost every conversation we had.

It was monsoon and the Ecovillage was enveloped in vibrantly green foliage. The overcast conditions, soft patter of the rains and the smell of fresh earth simply enhanced the beauty of this rural landscape. What's more, we had the exciting opportunity to work in the paddy fields alongside the local farmers. The conducive ambience facilitated an experience that led to an increased absorption in the Gita, and a wonderful contemplation and assimilation of its teachings. Soon, the lustre of the city comforts appeared to be fading away amidst this rural setting.

An organic ambience facilitates easier assimilation and contemplation of spiritual wisdom.

A Reflection on Transition

One mesmerizing sight at the Ecovillage was the Kohoj mountain. We would marvel at its magnificence from any spot of the Ecovillage and especially from the terrace of our two-storey ashram building. Bathed in the showers of the monsoon, the mountain would adorn itself with bright green vegetation. Drifting clouds would occasionally veil the mountain, while milky waterfalls would make its smooth rocks glisten. This was a sight I loved to behold.

Months passed, and the season transitioned from monsoon to autumn, and slowly the mountain transformed. What was once a beautiful green spectacle gradually turned brown and dusty. With winter's arrival, the mountain assumed a dry appearance, giving me an opportunity to reflect on one of the very first lessons we learnt from the Bhagavad-Gita (2.14).

mātrā-sparśās tu kaunteya
śītoṣṇa-sukha-duhkha-dāh
āgamāpāyino 'nityās
tāṁs titikṣasva bhārata

Lord Krishna spoke to His dear friend Arjuna: 'O son of Kuntī, whenever the senses interact with the sense objects, sensations of cold and heat, and happiness and distress arise. These dualities appear and disappear like the winter and summer seasons, and are transient in nature. One must learn to tolerate (*titiksha*) such temporary dualities without being disturbed.'

Having lived at Govardhan Ecovillage for about fifteen years now, I observed the cyclical transformation of the Kohoj mountain every year—a fleeting green beauty and a transient dryness. This natural rhythm mirrors the temporary nature of happiness and sadness in life, similar to the changing seasons.

Addressing the Common Question

People often approach me with a burning question: 'How do I deal with life's troubles and distressing situations?'

In response, I try giving them solace quoting the above Gita *shloka*. My advice to them is to *embrace tolerance in the face of adversity*, apart from doing whatever is practically feasible. This tolerance isn't a passive resignation from addressing the problems; rather, it involves giving our best to navigate life's challenges.

We need to try our best to avoid difficulties in life as far as humanly possible. But if, despite our efforts, the situation persists, then the key is to learn to live with it, and find the opportunity to grow within the unsurpassable boundaries set by the situations.

Three compelling reasons support this idea of tolerance.

1. *Purpose*: First and foremost, *there is a purpose behind every occurrence*. Despite our attempts to ward off a situation, its persistence suggests a greater purpose at play. Sometimes, life's most distressful events can later turn out to be the most significant and foundational moments for future happiness. We can realize this in retrospect.

2. *Transience*: The second reason is that *life's happiness and distress are transient*, akin to the changing seasons. Overly succumbing to any adversity can hinder us from fully embracing life. Recognizing the temporary nature of distress allows us to gracefully endure and grow.
3. *Appreciation*: The third reason to embrace tolerance is elegantly simple. Can we truly savour the sweetness of life without experiencing its bitterness? The answer is no. Navigating and enduring through life's challenging moments helps us *genuinely appreciate life's joys*. Embracing distress allows us to revel in true happiness when delightful circumstances eventually unfold.

In line with the above reasons to tolerate, try to reflect on the following:

1. Reflect on moments when you encountered distress but later recognized its importance as life unfolded.
2. Have you ever experienced relief and liberation from pain by meditating on the temporary nature of a difficulty?
3. Envision savouring six different types of sweets sequentially; then compare that experience to eating a sweet immediately after burning your mouth with a hot chilli.

In summary, practising tolerance involves understanding the greater purpose behind challenges, acknowledging the temporary nature of distress, and appreciating the contrast

between joy and sorrow that makes life's sweetness truly fulfilling.

The art of acceptance and tolerance makes life's journey less exhausting and more exciting.

The Transient Nature of Pleasure and Pain

I have seen this fundamental, yet profound wisdom actionable numerous times in my own life and the lives of many around me. Just as we employ measures to shield ourselves from the heat and cold, we must cultivate the ability to endure and grow through the joys and sorrows in life.

In the intricate tapestry of human experience, we often derive pleasure from a myriad of sources—be it the glow of success, or the allure of physical charm. Yet, a stark reality underlies these moments of joy: none of these sources bestow a permanent sense of fulfilment. Their temporary nature becomes apparent with the passage of time. Bodily beauty, once a source of delight, erodes with time. Similarly, the pinnacle of success we might attain could seem insignificant at a later point in time. In this way, pain also can't live on with time. Personal failures, physical sickness and natural calamities hurt us like storms. But the good news is that no storm stays forever. So, learn the art of tolerance.

Imagine standing on the shores of an ocean, observing its swelling waves rise during high tides. How long do they hold up? Well, they swiftly recede within moments,

isn't it? Similar are life's pleasures and pains—fleeting like the waves of an ocean, rising and falling. Eventually, we will find both of them weakened and faded with time. The solution to a wonderful life is embracing the natural flow of pains and pleasures. Acknowledging their transient nature provides us the inspiration to endure without being overwhelmed.

No pain or pleasure can stay forever, so learn to endure.

Life is like a journey in a vast ocean. Do you want to be a mere passenger tossed by the waves of dualities? Or a resilient navigator steering your course with a profound understanding of the impermanence that surrounds you? The choice is yours!

Now, you may think, 'I understand the transient nature of happiness and distress. I need to tolerate pain and be resilient in failures. But tolerating pleasure or success makes no sense to me. Although short-lived, beauty, success and victory give me joy. Should I not celebrate them? Should I be deprived of the self-evident pleasures of life by understanding their temporary nature?'

Here is a response to your questions!

Role of Rejoice and Regret

Rejoicing in success and regretting failure are the natural responses of most individuals. But the Gita holds something special for all of us. It teaches us to work on balancing our responses. Because, it is our response to

sweet and bitter experiences that shape the narrative of our lives.

It is natural and necessary to embrace moments of success, but that success shouldn't lead to complacency, recklessness, overconfidence, pride or arrogance. We can rejoice in success with humility and gratitude, avoiding the pitfalls of pride and overexcitement.

Likewise, in the face of personal failures and hardships, lamenting and succumbing to disappointment, discouragement and depression is not the best choice. Instead, we must honestly repent for our mistakes that caused the failure, and try to rectify them while being careful not to repeat them.

> *Happy moments, if unchecked, may lead to overconfidence and pride, while distressful moments can induce depression and dysfunction. Tolerate the urge to be overexcited by temporary happiness or disheartened by fleeting distress.*

It is through this understanding and resilience that we can derive true fulfilment amidst the impermanence of life's ever-changing landscape. In short, here are two glowing keys to grow through success and failure:

> *Celebrate success with gratitude, avoiding pitfalls of pride and overexcitement.*
>
> *Endure failure with resilience, avoiding disappointment and depression.*

Also, try to reflect on one of your biggest successes, identify a major contributor (other than yourself) and appreciate

their contribution. Reflect on one of your biggest setbacks and identify the greatest learning it delivered to you.

Relish the Transience

The solution to a wonderful life is embracing the natural flow of pain and pleasure. In fact, it's the constantly moving waves that make a water body beautiful. Stagnant water stinks but running water nourishes life. Let's not expect life to be stagnant by desiring a comfort zone. Let's allow life's ups and downs to help us grow and glow with inner strength. Let's transcend the temporary fluctuations of life by tolerance, but also learn to relish the transience with resilience. The winter cold, summer heat or drenching monsoon may cause discomfort, but they do bring us some delight in their own way.

At Govardhan Ecovillage, I experienced the ferocity of three seasons, but I also learnt to relish them. The chilling winter did bring about some trouble, but we found joy in the cosiness of bundling up in warm layers, indulging in hot beverages and rejoicing in the season's charm. The scorching summer sun did bake our backs, but we thoroughly enjoyed extended hours of warm sunlight, pleasant mornings and evenings, along with breathtaking sunrises and sunsets. Our clothes did take longer to dry during the monsoons, but the revitalizing rainfall, the aroma of wet soil, lush greenery and blooming flora charmed our hearts. Above all, we relished making offerings of seasonal flowers and food to our dear Lordships in the temple, while celebrating spiritual seasonal festivals with great joy and enthusiasm.

Just like any season has two faces—the exhausting face and the exciting face, any experience in life has two sides—the tiring side and the thrilling side. Pleasures may distract us, pains may dishearten us, but for one who embraces tolerance, growing amidst all the inevitable dualities of life becomes a piece of cake.

Life's amazing quest lies in discovering moments of sweetness amidst challenging experiences.

The Kohoj mountain near our Govardhan Ecovillage stood steady, strong, immovable and unaffected, amidst all the seasonal changes that brought variegated climates of intense cold, scorching heat and heavy rains. Similarly, a mature person equipped with tolerance remains steady and unaffected by the ups and downs of this world, and stays calm amidst chaos.

Think about this: Do we experience the same joy one year after having received an appraisal at work as we did on the day we received it? Do we see people experience the same intensity of grief after having lost a dear one, years later in their life? Life moves on. Learning to go and grow through life's offerings makes life an amazing experience. So, I hope you are prepared to experience a life-changing embrace—an embrace called tolerance.

Should I Tolerate Injustice Too?

One final question: 'While it may be reasonable to tolerate pains and pleasures in life, is it both possible and necessary to tolerate the injustices we face? What if people deliberately

trouble us? What if they exploit our good nature for their gain? Should we tolerate such behaviour?'

The answer is a resounding 'No'. If people cause trivial inconveniences accidentally, we can tolerate and excuse them, but if they are intent on misbehaving with us, we must respond suitably.

On the battlefield of Kurukshetra, Arjuna faced a dilemma while preparing to combat his own family members. He pondered, 'How can I lead a joyful life if I kill my own relatives? The absence of my dear ones would diminish the joy of palace comforts and a prosperous kingdom.'

Lord Krishna responded to Arjuna's dilemma with wisdom: 'Dear Arjuna, one who is born must certainly die. Death of near and dear ones certainly causes pain, but one must tolerate such pains in the performance of one's duties' (BG 2.27).

While Lord Krishna advised Arjuna to tolerate the pain of losing relatives, He never advocated tolerating the injustice perpetrated by them. Earlier, when Arjuna declined to fight with his own relatives on the grounds of family bonds, Lord Krishna condemned his emotions and sentiments as petty weakness of heart.

Emotions are natural, but being excessively emotional is harmful.

How would Lord Krishna, the proponent of *dharma* (virtue), allow *adharma* (vice) to flourish? He disallowed Arjuna from tolerating the injustices of wicked Duryodhana and his supporters. Lord Krishna told Arjuna, 'Give up this

weakness of heart. Abandon this feeble hesitation and rise to the battle without lethargy' (BG 3.30).

Give Tolerance Eyes

Understanding when to apply the principle of tolerance and setting limits is crucial. Lord Krishna was not contradicting Himself by promoting both tolerance and fighting with relatives. Lord Krishna imparts a logical lesson:

> *While we must tolerate life's inevitable dualities of pains and pleasures, tolerating deliberate injustice and inappropriate behaviour is unwarranted.*
>
> *Those with the ability and responsibility to rectify injustice should not silently witness it; such passive tolerance is a weakness. Conversely, tolerating the inherent challenges and pressures of life is indicative of a strong heart.*

A balanced understanding of kindness and firmness is necessary. Lord Krishna teaches the profound lesson that appropriately punishing wrongdoers is also an act of kindness. Without such fitting punishment, wrongdoers are likely to repeat their mistakes instead of learning from them.

In conclusion, we must try to tolerate the inevitable dualities in life, but not deliberate injustices and inappropriate behaviours. That's the mature application of tolerance for a balanced life.

Give tolerance eyes. Blind tolerance may be hazardous.

Practices for Inner Balance

1. *Reflect on Life's Dualities:* Contemplate the transient nature of both pleasure and pain, to not get overwhelmed by them. Identify distressful moments that later turned out to be beneficial as life unfolded.
2. *Maintain Balanced Reactions:* While it's natural to rejoice in success and regret failure, avoid overconfidence in success and resist succumbing to despair in failure.
3. *Celebrate Success with Humility:* Acknowledge the contributions of friends and well-wishers who assisted you in attaining success. Be grateful and avoid the pitfalls of pride, overexcitement and complacency.
4. *Navigate Challenges with Resilience:* In the face of personal failures and hardships, practise honest self-reflection, regret any mistakes, but don't succumb to despair. Learn from failures and grow with hope and determination.
5. *Relish Life's Transience:* Embrace the natural flow of life's pleasures and pains that contributes to the beauty of life, much like the constantly moving waves in a water body or delightful seasonal changes.
6. *Apply Tolerance with Discernment:* Tolerate the temporary dualities and unintentional mistakes, not deliberate injustices and offences. Take appropriate action towards exploitation.

3

Soaring above Life's Traffic

Fostering Equanimity by Elevating Life's Purpose

Once, I had to board a morning flight from Mumbai. Although I started early from the Ecovillage, I was caught up in a traffic bottleneck for nearly an hour. Thoughts of the flight taking off without me were haunting me and so at one point in time, I got out of the car.

Then, I began walking to a spot that was somewhat less congested and tried hailing a cab. I thought this would save me a lot of time and prevent my boarding pass from turning into a useless piece of paper. Unfortunately, time had other plans and so did the multitude of cab drivers who whizzed past me.

Hard-pressed, I continued to walk, crossing lanes and dodging vehicles, until finally, I happened to find an autorickshaw at a relatively less congested part of the road. Wasting no time, I jumped in but within a few minutes,

my phone began to ring. It was my driver, he had somehow managed to squeeze through the clog and was on his way to pick me up.

I got out of the rickshaw and hastily entered the car. Once again, I faced the onslaught of red traffic lights that appeared to be taking forever to turn green. Soon the car was swerving and swaying from left to right, but eventually, I made it to the airport just in time.

Fortunately, check-in wasn't quite as rushed, and travelling with no baggage proved to be an added advantage. I smoothly cut through the security and headed straight to the seating area close to the boarding gate, with about thirty minutes to spare.

Soon, I boarded the aircraft, and as it launched into the sky, I looked out at the city down below—the skyscrapers, roads, cars, buses, local trains, junctions and traffic lights. Everything looked so tiny. My car had to stop at red lights, slither through a perpetual queue of vehicles and acrobatically manoeuvre through vehicular cobwebs that dotted the street. But thousands of miles up above, far away from the rules of the road, I was now cruising through the clouds while sipping some fruit juice. What relevance did the chaos below now have? The experience left me thinking.

Now let me share something that may switch the way you see things in life. This experience of mine has a connection with the challenges we face in life. And how's that? Well, when we elevate our intelligence and consciousness to a higher level, our seemingly huge problems of life appear tiny and insignificant, as we simply fly over them.

Elevate yourself to a higher plane to transcend the trivial issues on the lower plane.

So, what do we do?

Equanimity for Inner Peace

This airplane-like mindset that enables us to soar above the dualities of life is technically called equanimity or *samatva*, which Lord Krishna emphasizes in the Gita (2.15): '*sama-duhkha-sukham dhīram*—A wise person is equipoised towards the inevitable joys and sorrows of life.'

In life's journey, we often face many roadblocks and red signals of difficulties and distresses. Just as green and red signals on the road cannot affect an airplane's movement, someone endowed with equanimity on the basis of spiritual wisdom isn't affected by the dualities of joy and sorrow, or success and failure in life. Equanimity involves achieving a state of neutrality and detachment from life's trivial dualities, by directing our focus towards a higher purpose or improved ways of living.

Equanimity is that airplane that elevates you beyond the green signals of joys and red signals of sorrows.

Lord Krishna beautifully explains this secret of equanimity in duality in the Bhagavad-Gita (2.38):

sukha-duhkhe same kṛtvā
lābhālābhau jayājayau

'Dear Arjuna, perform your duty without being swayed by happiness or distress, gain or loss, victory or defeat.'

By being equipoised towards the fluctuations of joy and sorrow, we can experience a profound sense of tranquillity. In such a state of mind, our response to life's situations would be effective, free of impulsive reactions and embedded in rational decision-making.

Every problem in life doesn't always have a solution; that's where equanimity comes to the rescue. Problems that are meant to be overlooked shouldn't be 'overly' looked at, only to make you feel overwhelmed and dysfunctional. So, adopt this practice and see the magic of peace it creates in your mind.

'But what is the exact process that we need to follow?' Good question. Let's uncover the answer.

The Process: A Meeting with Equanimity

We all yearn to secure a ticket to 'Equanimity Airlines' where we can experience peace and remain undisturbed amidst trivial inconveniences. Fortunately, the price for purchasing the ticket is not a million dollars.

1. **Build a Purpose**

   The first step to boarding that airline involves cultivating a purpose in life, followed by developing a taste for that purpose. Let me elaborate.

   Consider someone battling a junk food addiction, aiming to break free. To conquer this challenge, they must foster a strong purpose and

a profound desire for a healthier life. Once they establish this purpose and desire for a healthy lifestyle, they naturally find the inspiration to free themselves from the allure of junk food. But what sustains this purpose? A higher taste.

After relishing the nourishment and vitality of a healthy lifestyle, they are naturally motivated to steadfastly adhere to their new-found purpose. Thus, their purpose of living a healthier life, fuelled by the taste they experienced by taking to such a life, inspires them to win over the junk food temptation.

This very principle applies to our lives as well. We need to have a purpose in life. For that, we need to cultivate self-awareness. There are multiple facets of this term 'self-awareness', but let me highlight one fundamental aspect of it.

> *Self-awareness:* We are spiritual beings living within material bodies in this world. The bodies are temporary and subject to change, but the person within the body, the spirit soul, is eternal, a child of God, the eternal father of all beings. When the present body is old, dead or destroyed, the soul within the body passes into another body. Being conscious of our eternal spiritual and temporary material identities is called 'self-awareness'.

This is one of the initial lessons that Lord Krishna imparted in the Gita. With self-awareness, we need to focus on the two main purposes of life: (1) the immediate purpose of self-preservation, and (2) the ultimate purpose of self-realization. Now let us see what exactly they are.

1. *Self-preservation:* Although the material body is temporary, as long as we live within the body, it's our responsibility to work for the maintenance of the body, do justice to all the roles and designations acquired with the body, and protect all the bodily possessions; of course, with a spirit of detachment because one day we have to leave them all. This is called 'self-preservation'—the immediate purpose of life.
2. *Self-realization:* Knowing that we all are spiritual beings beyond the bodily designations, we need to engage ourselves in spiritual practices to realize our spiritual identity. Spiritual practices include worship, meditation, prayer, hearing about the Lord and chanting His names, and so on. All these spiritual activities help us realize our relationship with God and strengthen our loving bonding with Him, which is called 'self-realization'—the ultimate purpose of life.

Our focus on the trio of self-awareness, self-preservation and self-realization makes our life's course meaningful, purposeful and fulfilling even amidst the inevitable chaos of this external world.

A spiritual purpose allows us to focus on the permanent amidst the temporary, enabling us to remain in the world but not get affected by it.

When we practise spiritual living, we naturally develop a taste for it, because we are inherently spiritual beings and spiritual life is naturally very joyful to us. Upon savouring the blissful essence of spiritual life, it naturally becomes our life's purpose and desired goal. Then, equipped with a spiritual purpose, we can gracefully soar above life's challenges without succumbing to them.

Let me share another story to illustrate this point further.

2. **Stick to the Higher Taste**
   During a family shopping trip in my early teens, I joined my little cousin and her mom at a store. While her mother explored, the five-year-old became captivated by a pricey toy phone that played songs. She asked her mom for it, but cleverly, her mom offered her own Nokia phone. The girl insisted on the toy, leading to a comical argument about its impracticality. Seeing the child's tears and a commotion, I intervened and suggested giving in to her wishes, and eventually, her mom relented.

Returning to the shop, the girl struggled to pick a colour for her toy but settled on pink. Her mom, indifferent to colour, paid promptly, prioritizing time. The child happily pressed the keys of her chosen toy, and the shopping episode, marked by humour and a happy resolution, concluded with the child enjoying her new possession.

Reflecting on this incident, I learnt a powerful lesson about the importance of cultivating a purpose or a higher taste. It highlighted the ability to soar above life's dualities, much like an airplane untouched by turbulence. The innocent child, caught up in colour choices, lacked the perspective of the experienced mother. The seasoned mother, having already obtained a functional phone, remained indifferent to the toy's colour intricacies. Having tasted the satisfaction of possessing a real phone, she effortlessly transcended the dilemma of choosing among various toy phone colours. This teaches us a profound lesson:

> *By embracing a higher taste and dedicating ourselves to a noble purpose, we can maintain a serene neutrality amidst life's trivialities and dualities.*

3. Rise above Lower Tastes

Equanimity is not an inability to differentiate between dualities, but an ability to remain unaffected by them. It is a virtue that eases even

the toughest situations loaded with bias, prejudice and attachment.

Equanimity is not meant to promote irresponsibility or insensitivity—just as the mother acknowledged the innocent attachments and choices of the child, yet remained neutral and unaffected by the toy's colour.

Having a rational mindset doesn't imply ignoring the other's emotion.

Emphasizing the significance of developing a higher purpose in life, Lord Krishna says in the Gita (2.59): '*param dṛṣṭvā nivartate*—One can successfully rise above lower tastes by cultivating a higher taste.'

Sometimes, children engage in the delightful ritual of building sandcastles on the beach during picnics with their parents. As the rhythmic sea waves gently lap the shore, elders absorb themselves in light-hearted or profound discussions about life, while the children immerse themselves in the creation of intricate sand structures. Reflecting on my own childhood, I recall burying my foot in the sand, skillfully extracting it to form a sandy cave, and adorning it with leaves and twigs.

But then, when parents eventually call their children to leave the beach and return home, the little ones reluctantly abandon their sandy creations, showcasing an innocent attachment to their temporary homes. However, the parents, with

a broader perspective, understand the transient nature of these sandy abodes and gently guide their kids towards their real home.

Similarly, as we mature, our life's purpose tends to ascend, causing us to adopt a more elevated viewpoint. This doesn't imply indecisiveness or indifference towards life's situations but rather *a mature outlook that recognizes their relative insignificance in the context of a higher purpose and mission in life.* This cultivated equanimity becomes an invaluable asset, enabling us to navigate life's inevitable highs and lows in an unthinkable way.

The material world often urges us to live life as it unfolds, as prolonged contemplation on a spiritual purpose might entangle us in a web of rules and regulations. Yes! We can live life as it unfolds, but we need to tether it to a higher purpose—a spiritual purpose that doesn't impose rules and rituals, but helps us enter into a state of happiness and peace by freeing us from the impact of the world's stress and tensions.

Practices for Inner Balance

1. *Upgrade Your Life's Purpose:* Regularly evaluate your life's goals. As priorities shift, focus on higher purposes, and rise above petty problems that seem serious but may be trivial in the grander scheme of life.
2. *Embrace a Higher Taste:* Cultivate a noble purpose beyond immediate desires, and rise above life's trivialities and dualities, akin to an airplane untouched by turbulence.
3. *Rise above Lower Tastes:* Cultivate detachment, equanimity and a rational mindset that eases even the toughest situations loaded with bias and prejudice.
4. *Focus on the Trio of Life:* With self-awareness, strive for the two purposes of life, namely self-preservation and self-realization, to make your life course meaningful and fulfilling.
5. *Tether Life to a Spiritual Purpose:* Live life as it unfolds but tether it to a higher, spiritual purpose, that doesn't just impose rules and rituals but leads to genuine happiness and peace, freeing you from the tensions of the world.

4

Possessed by Possessions!

Life's Fleeting Moments and Detached Living

Once, I was travelling in a train from Pune to Mumbai, two well-known Indian cities. I had a reserved berth, luckily a window seat. Soon, the train tooted its departure, and the buzzing station passed into the distance. Slowly, the locomotive entered a thickly vegetated region.

This was Lonavala. A hilly terrain offering a spectacular view of rolling hills covered in a blanket of green. Gurgling waterfalls adorn this area during the monsoon. I saw the valleys, mountains, trees, sky, sun, clouds, flowers and plants—all from the tiny window. As I beheld the beauty of nature, my stomach demanded my attention and soon, I was sending in a steady supply of snacks lovingly packed by my mother. All this while, the breeze had been doing its thing, caressing my face and carrying the aroma of the goodies that safely rested in my lunchbox.

I started reflecting on how such a wonderful scene provided delight to my eyes, yet it quickly passed by. Captivating visuals vanish quickly, just like the fast-moving train reveals landscapes only for a fleeting moment. As the train trudged on, my eyes caught a beautiful tree adorned with colourful flowers. Intrigued, I tried to look again through the window and asked my friend about the tree and flower, but he didn't notice it, and in no time, they had disappeared into thin air.

Isn't life similar, where we embark on individual journeys, encountering people, places, positions, possessions, excitements, exhaustions and diverse results of our activities that just pass by in moments? None of these are permanent; we can't hold on to anything forever. Life keeps moving, and moments, whether happy or sad, and the results of our activities, whether small or big, are fleeting.

Memories may linger in our minds for a long time, but the moments themselves pass away.

This realization made me appreciate the profound message of *detachment* in the Bhagavad-Gita. The Gita teaches the art of detachment from our possessions, positions, privileges and variegated results of our activities, but while fully committing to our duties. It may seem contradictory, but with a little analysis, the profound truths of this foundational lesson become apparent. Let's explore the message together.

The Art of Smart Work

Therefore, Lord Krishna gives this golden advice on balancing detachment and responsibility. Lord Krishna teaches us the art of smart work in the Bhagavad-Gita (2.47) as follows:

karmaṇy evādhikāras te
mā phaleṣu kadācana
mā karma-phala-hetur bhūr
mā te sango 'stv akarmaṇi

This verse has four parts:

1. You have a right to perform your duty
2. You are not entitled to the results
3. Never consider yourself the cause of the results of your activities
4. Never give up your duties or responsibilities

Essentially, they teach us that we have the right and responsibility to perform our duties to the best of our capacity. But we have no control over the results, and therefore we need to be detached, not from the work but from its results.

Be dedicated to your duties, and detached from the outcomes they produce.

Two Sides of Detachment

Detachment manifests in two forms.

1. *Detachment Before Work*: The first facet of detachment is to be cultivated before taking up any work. Oftentimes, people work with predetermined expectations, such as aiming for top exam scores or anticipating massive success in a creative project. Reasonable aspirations are acceptable, but undue expectation of specific results must be avoided.
2. *Detachment After Work*: The second facet of detachment is to be demonstrated after work. For instance, we have amassed great wealth by sincere efforts, and constructed an impressive building or acquired a car. We can responsibly maintain these possessions, and shouldn't be too possessive about them, but be detached.

Do the above two sides of detachment make much sense to you fully? Isn't it an irony? 'If I work so hard, why should I be detached from the results of my work—either past results or future results?' The simple answer is: 'To avoid frustration!'

Adjust Expectations, Avoid Frustrations

Yes! Undue expectations often lead to frustration when the expectations are unfulfilled. Undoubtedly, aspirations are the architects of our dreams, and ambitions drive us to work with dedication. However, when these dreams

transform into unrealistic expectations about how swiftly success should materialize, how great the results must be or how the world should perceive us, the burden intensifies.

The weight of impractical expectations, whether imposed by oneself or projected by others, becomes burdensome, paving the way for disappointment, discouragement and even the shadows of depression. The journey from 'reasonable plans' to 'unreasonable expectations' is deceitful, laden with the potential for emotional upheaval.

Embracing the spirit of detachment and regulating expectations save us from frustrations in work and relationships.

Freedom from Possessiveness

Coming to the second facet of detachment mentioned above, when external factors like financial crises or emergencies force us to part with the possessions we accumulated with hard work, we won't be able to digest it without cultivating a spirit of detachment.

In times of economic downturns, individuals faced with unemployment may need to relinquish holdings or assets. It's crucial not to overly identify oneself with the possessions accumulated by past endeavours, as clinging to these achievements can lead to profound sadness when circumstances dictate letting go.

Ultimately, one day, we have to give up proprietorship over all our properties at the time of death. Death separates us from all our properties, achievement and possessions,

and even from our own body. And the sad news is that no one can avoid death, however influential and accomplished one may be.

At the time of death, no material wealth accompanies us, emphasizing the transient nature of possessions acquired through dedicated efforts. Therefore, cultivating the spirit of detachment is mandatory.

Problems with a Result-driven Mindset

The problems with a result-driven mindset are:

1. Arrogance when results meet expectations
2. Depression when results are below expectations
3. Compromise of values to attain expected results

Unmet expectations breed depression, while their fulfilment might lead to arrogance.

For instance, consider two people who want to grow their social media presence.

One of them ardently seeks elevated numbers—views, likes and followers—by hook or by crook, resorting to artificial means that inflate follower counts but lack authenticity. This path may deceive onlookers, impressing them momentarily with inflated figures.

On the other hand, the other person, driven by a genuine desire to impact lives positively, shares inspiring content on social media to add value to lives. This person's joy is found not in the pursuit of numbers but in the heartfelt connections made and the transformative impact achieved. They relish the process, finding fulfilment in the

honesty and integrity of their efforts, and are satisfied with whatever results they obtain. For such a person, there is no arrogance in obtaining great numbers, no depression or compromise in values when fewer numbers are attained.

When fixated on outcomes, one may succumb to the allure of shortcuts, sacrificing authenticity for superficial gains. However, a value-conscious approach prioritizes integrity over numbers, leading to inner fulfilment. In the pursuit of noble goals, the genuine individual thrives, leaving a lasting impact on those touched by their sincere endeavours.

Social Distancing from Outcomes

While it is commendable to invest substantial effort and dedication in the pursuit of one's goals, it is equally crucial to recognize the tipping point where dedication in work transforms into attachment to results.

Responsibility shouldn't lead to undue attachment; and detachment shouldn't lead to irresponsibility. After giving our best, the key lies in stepping back, creating a healthy distance from the outcome. Detachment, in this context, is not a relinquishment of ambition but a strategic retreat to safeguard emotional well-being.

Detachment is not a renunciation of hard work but a wise and necessary measure to shield ourselves from the emotional toll of unrealistic expectations. By navigating the delicate balance between aspiration and detachment, we pave the way for a more resilient and contented journey towards our goals.

Detachment serves as a shield against the relentless onslaught of frustration.

It's not that we become detached when we attain unpleasant results, but beginning our work with a detached mindset saves us from being affected by unpleasant results.

Detachment shouldn't be an outcome of frustration, but should be a saviour from frustration.

Not that we shouldn't care for results, but we should care more for our internal inspiration. Unless we are sufficiently motivated or inspired to do good work, we don't have the scope to bounce back when there are setbacks. Motivation is the most essential asset for us to move ahead in the life journey of self-improvement. If one setback or an unpleasant result demotivates us to work further, where is the scope for another attempt?

Inspiration—The Real Asset

We work not only to produce results, but to improve ourselves, to learn, to grow and to attain fulfilment of our heart. We try to be detached from results to become attached to something better than results—self-enrichment.

When we choose to do a fulfilling activity, and invest our heart and soul into it, whether we attain an attention-attracting result or not, we will be happy. But if we are more result-oriented, sometimes, we become so obsessed with the results, that by hook or by crook, we want to attain results.

As long as we have a positive mindset, we can always strive for a better result next time. We cannot take charge of producing impressive results, but we need to take charge of our inner motivation and inspiration to do something worthwhile. If we become demotivated by one failure and thus develop a negative mindset, we can't work for our betterment. That's why no exciting result is worth risking our motivation. Detachment protects us from falling into negative emotions when facing setbacks in life.

To protect the real asset of motivation, let's cultivate a detached mindset over a result-driven mindset.

Pertinently, Lord Krishna recommends in the Bhagavad-Gita that we work with detachment. Equipped with detachment, we can stay steady amidst disappointments, learn what we can from the situations and move on.

If we become demotivated by unpleasant results, then we miss the opportunity to rejoice in the sincere effort we put into our work. We need to also learn to enjoy the journey while reaching the destination.

Do your best, and be detached from the outcome.

Combining Responsibility and Detachment

Let's come back to the train journey. When we travel in a train, we have the facilities of a reserved berth with lights, fans, attached toilet and scenic views from the window. Still, we face multiple inconveniences like delays, hubbub, catering interruptions, food sellers' intermittent

announcements and congested berths. Despite all that, the journey offers us the opportunities of personal time, contemplation, interactions with nice fellow passengers and so on.

As long as we are on the journey, we can enjoy the facilities, take the benefit of the opportunities and must tolerate the inconveniences. But as soon as our destination arrives, we must get down from the train, leaving all the facilities and opportunities of the train behind. None of them were permanent. Even if we are attached to the scenic beauty seen through the window, we must still alight. But of course, the good news is that we leave all the inconveniences of the train behind too.

Similarly, our life journeys also present several facilities, opportunities, possessions, positions and several difficulties as well. But none of them are permanent, and are like the passing scenery seen through the train window. The difference is that a train journey lasts for a few hours, and life's journey lasts for a few decades. So, it is justified and is repeatedly recommended in the Gita and many other wisdom texts that we cultivate the mentality of *detachment*.

All the facilities, opportunities and inconveniences in our journey, whether in a train or in life, are transient.

However, in the name of detachment, we cannot be irresponsible in our lives. We must do justice to all the roles and designations we hold. We must be responsible towards all the duties we take up. Although we may need to get down at our destination, isn't it my responsibility to keep

my berth and surroundings clean, be polite with fellow passengers and not create any disturbances?

Many times, people who travel in public transport like buses and trains, tend to be irresponsible towards their surroundings. They may not flush the toilets, they may throw garbage around, waste electricity, be indifferent to co-passengers, mishandle seats, lights, fans, switches and so on. Therefore, the concerned authorities often display signages encouraging cleanliness, politeness and respect, and even extract fines from those who violate certain protocols and etiquettes. After all, everything is transient; no one stays in a bus, train or railway station eternally, and no one can take away anything from there—yet responsible and careful behaviour is expected.

Detachment ≠ Irresponsibility
Responsibility ≠ Possessiveness

Similarly, we need to be responsible towards our transient duties and designations in life, but without being overly attached to them, knowing very well that we have to leave all of them one day. The more attached we are to our positions and possessions, the more vulnerable we become to potential suffering due to possessiveness.

While we need to be responsible towards our positions and possessions, excessive attachment leads to troubles, when we have to inevitably leave them one day.

Practices for Inner Balance

1. *Perform Your Duties with Dedication*: Strive to do your best in every task you undertake, understanding that your duty is in your control, but the results are not.
2. *Adjust Expectations, Avoid Frustrations*: Set realistic and attainable goals, and save yourself from emotional upheavals caused by undue expectations.
3. *Cultivate Freedom from Possessiveness*: While enjoying the fruits of your labour, avoid becoming overly possessive. Recognize that external factors or changes may require you to let go of certain possessions.
4. *Cultivate a Value-Conscious Approach*: In the pursuit of your goals, avoid compromising your principles, and prioritize genuine connections and positive impact over superficial gains.
5. *Protect Your Motivation*: Cultivate a mindset that prioritizes inner inspiration over external outcomes, and focus on the fulfilling activity regardless of the results.
6. *Combine Responsibility and Detachment*: Acknowledge the transient nature of facilities, opportunities and difficulties in life's journey, and embrace detachment without neglecting your responsibilities.

5

From Confusion to Clarity

The Adventure of Seeking Wise Counsel

I was once on a trip to Kanchipuram, a holy place located in Tamil Nadu, one of the southern states of India. With my companions alongside, we were heading to the sacred site by car. And behind the wheel was one of our Tamil-speaking friends.

That day, we planned to visit a particular ancient temple of Lord Vishnu, generally called Divya-desam, that would serve as an en route stopover while on our way to Kanchipuram. Now, although this friend of ours knew that area, he wasn't so sure of the temple's precise location.

Those were days when only one among us had a smartphone. Immediately, that friend pulled out his device and suggested that we make use of Google Maps to track down the temple. This was something new and exciting for me. He opened the app, typed in the location, and we

had an onscreen ETA (expected time of arrival) along with the route. I wondered at this marvel. Nowadays, it's quite common even for kids and grandmas to use this Global Positioning System but back then, it was my first exposure to G-Maps, the modern-day equivalent of a guiding light.

We had fuelled up the previous day, chosen our destination, planned our route meticulously, doing everything we could only so we could get to Kanchipuram on time. We were enjoying the ride, making light-hearted conversations and sharing smiles.

However, as we absorbed ourselves in this mirthful mood, our dear friend in the driver's seat took an inadvertent left turn, setting off on an unforeseen detour. Suddenly, the ETA bumped up. My friend quickly realized what he had done. 'The path hereon will involve multiple turns,' he said. 'Also, the lanes we'll get into are narrowly sandwiched and so are the muddy pathways that follow.'

These words struck me like a falling hammer. I was seeing all the effort and time spent in planning being flushed down the drain. So far, our banter had served as an engagement but now was the time to pay for all that entertainment. But, luckily for us, we quickly realized what we were up for. Time loss, sticky roads and hairpin bends; this was going to be tedious.

At that point, my friend spoke out. 'Someone should sit next to me with the Maps turned on and direct me as I drive. Now we must be even more careful with the cows and kids that roam about on the road.'

I immediately volunteered. With the newfound miracle (G-Maps) in my hand, I began guiding my friend through the twists and turns of the journey, when finally, we arrived at the grand temple that sat on the banks of a beautiful lake.

Just before we got out of the car, I shot a question at my friend. A question that had been buzzing through my head, the moment I familiarized myself with the GPS. 'What happens if we take a wrong turn with the map turned on?'

'Well, the moment you deviate from the right route, the map recalculates the optimal route, and shows you the next best path to your destination.'

Impressive, I thought. Isn't that the role of a true guide in life? Redirecting us to the right way, the instant we move off track?

That day, I realized something beautiful. It's a great fortune to have a mature guide in life, but a fortune still greater is approaching that guide in times of confusion.

What to Do When You Don't Know What to Do

Life is convoluted and distractions are bound to come. And at some point, we've all experienced an unexpected left turn and detour. But the difference is the name, that's all. Some call those turns mental chaos and conflicting thoughts, while others call them ethical dilemmas and relationship pullbacks.

The absence of a clear road map often leads us down uncharted paths in life. But here's a simple solution to

never get stuck, no matter the path you tread. I call this an *internal reboot.*

So, how exactly does this work? Well, all you have to do is simply seek guidance from an experienced well-wisher or mentor, enabling you to recalibrate your internal compass, and thereby redirecting you towards purpose and fulfilment.

Personally, this is one of my favourite practices, where I offload all the stress of finding a way out, and instead let a seasoned well-wisher guide me through the tangles. Try this and I would be glad to know how it worked for you.

Now allow me to present a scene from the ancient epic, the Bhagavad-Gita. Arjuna, a celebrated warrior, is seen grappling with profound internal conflicts and confusion on the battlefield of Kurukshetra. Arjuna knew it was his right to fight for his lawful share of the kingdom, but he did not know whether fighting against his own relatives and family was okay. He was indecisive, thinking to himself, 'Should I fight or not?'

Now this is not simply an example of indecisiveness, but a classic representation of the human condition of seeking clarity amidst confusion. What did Arjuna do then? He turned to his dear friend, well-wisher and guide, Lord Krishna. In a state of bewilderment, Arjuna maturely chose to seek Lord Krishna's guidance. This is real intelligence—knowing what to do when we don't know what to do! Something like our GPS.

Amidst life's dilemmas and times of turmoil, seeking guidance from an experienced well-wisher is beneficial.

When I learnt this system of internal rebooting, the first couple of questions that came to my mind were: 'Do I really need someone to guide me?', 'Can't I help myself on my own?' Well, let me share what I found . . .

Humility—The Mark of True Intelligence

A basic problem all of us face is a strong sense of self-righteousness. Often, our ego glamorizes individualism and independence: 'Be yourself, don't depend on others.' Of course, we need to be self-dependent to a considerable extent, because overdependence on others strangles our own creativity and thoughtfulness. In life, we need to equip ourselves with the necessary experience and wisdom to address the inevitable challenges. Yet, however learned we may be, there is always scope for learning more.

Give this a thought. What do you think overdependence on oneself can do? I feel it cuts us off from opportunities that grant us access to higher wisdom.

> *If we think we know a lot, we will be limited by what we know. But if we think we need to know a lot, this mindset will give us opportunities to grow and glow.*

A quick restart might help us cancel out functionality issues on our phone. But persistent device malfunctions may require the expertise of a technician. The solution to a mild headache may simply be adequate rest. However, when confronted with a significant health concern, relying on

self-treatment may prove to be inadequate, necessitating a consultation with a medical professional.

In the realm of life's intricate challenges, seeking assistance becomes imperative when confusion and chaos exceed one's resolution-finding capacity. Therefore, it is prudent to turn to individuals equipped with the capability to offer mature guidance and support.

> *When the magnitude of your problem outsizes the ability of your intelligence to find a solution, humbly approach a reliable guide for an answer. Such humility is the mark of true intelligence.*

Sometimes, we tend to think that we know the solution to our problem, and expect others to endorse it or at least assist us in implementing it. This is because we're more interested in seeking support from their hand, not head.

In contrast to this mindset, Arjuna expressed his condition to Lord Krishna in the Bhagavad-Gita (2.7) as follows:

kārpaṇya-doṣopahata-svabhāvah
pṛcchāmi tvām dharma-sammūḍha-cetāh
yac chreyah syān niścitam brūhi tan me
śiṣyas te 'ham śādhi mām tvām prapannam

'My mind is entangled in confusion about my duty. I have lost composure due to my weakness of heart. In this condition, I am asking You to please tell me for certain what is best for me. Now I am Your student surrendered unto You. Please instruct me.'

My Cup Is Full!

Arjuna exemplifies the mood of seeking guidance—humility and meekness. Such meekness in seeking guidance is not a weakness but a great strength. In this way, if we open ourselves to the prospect of seeking help, while parking our self-acclaiming mindset away, we inch forward to personal growth and find better solutions.

Admitting one's weakness is strength that gives us access to greater strength.

When we overestimate our intelligence, we underutilize the opportunity to benefit from a higher intelligence. So, mature guidance is vital for self-improvement. And that's the first lesson from the Bhagavad-Gita. We need to receive the counsel of an experienced guide with an open mind, stalling our ego, prejudice and preconceived notions. When your home-made techniques cannot address your sickness, you need to take advice from a reliable doctor, and follow it without arguments and doubts.

Think of a cup full of water. Can you pour milk or any kind of liquid into it without causing the contents to spill over?

True intelligence lies in seeking guidance from a reliable source, with an open mind!

But who is such a capable and reliable guide? How in the first place do we find one? What does an authentic guide look like? Does a guide have distinguishing marks on the

body or a stamp on the head? Well, the following is the answer you've been looking for.

Guide Detection

Amongst many remarkable qualities of one who qualifies to be a good guide, I highlight four vital ones below, based on what I understood from my life's experiences and how I received guidance in life.

1. *Well-wishing Nature:* The first distinctive quality of a guide is to be a genuine well-wisher. A genuineness check can filter out apparent well-wishers. And how do you carry out this test? Interact with the persons you consider to be your true well-wishers. Note how envious or non-envious they are of you. Then, identify how sincerely they rejoice in the success of those they guide. Also watch out for any taint of self-interest in their dealings with the ones they guide. At the end of this test, you would have found a genuine well-wisher.

   A good guide is a genuine well-wisher, free from envy.

2. *Practical Experience:* Sometimes we may find a well-wisher who empathizes with our problems, but can't really offer a concrete solution. This may be due to a lack of practical experience. So, look out for seasoned people who can provide practical solutions. Please note that you can have multiple

guides to help you in different aspects of your life. For solving day-to-day issues or professional dilemmas, you may consult guides who are experts in those fields, but while seeking guidance in your personal life and spiritual practices, you need mature guides.

3. *Emotional Sensitivity:* We may have found a genuine well-wisher who has tons of experience but what if they really can't understand our emotions? Well, it's vitally important that we choose an emotionally sensitive person as our guide.

> *A good guide provides both emotional support and rational advice.*

4. *Empowerment:* Sometimes, a guide may address a problem externally, or help us reconcile it internally. Not every problem under the sky has a solution, but whether there is a solution or not, we shouldn't lose our morale and inspiration to move on in life. Mature guides play a key role in protecting our motivation, which is more crucial than addressing the integrities of an issue on the ground. Such guides equip us with philosophical and spiritual perspectives to help us rise above the problem. Empowered by such mature counsel, we will soon begin to experience the manifestation of clarity in our mind, which is overwhelmed and bewildered by the issue at hand. In the end, we will be able to unleash our inherent potential and grow beyond our problems.

When resolving a problem is difficult, reconciling becomes practical.

5. *Connection*: Generally, one who is a good student of a subject can become its good teacher. Likewise, one who has received good guidance can become an effective guide. So, we need to look for spiritual guides who are strongly connected to their mature guides, who in turn had deep bonding with their respective guides. Authentic knowledge which originates from God is transparently transmitted through a chain of loyal teachers and students, and when we get connected to this chain, we can be assured of the quality of guidance we are receiving.

Life's journey becomes enriching with a well-wishing guide capable of comprehending our emotions, providing rational counsel and whatever solutions are humanly possible.

The hallmark of a true guide is the ability to balance emotion, rationality and practicality.

Illuminate Your Path

In the grand tapestry of life, the need for guidance is both universal and timeless. Arjuna found guidance in Lord Krishna and His wisdom in the Bhagavad-Gita. Similarly, today, turning to the same divine source can help us navigate life's complexities. The wisdom gained from

a genuine guide serves not only to navigate but also to enrich our journey with purpose and resilience.

After listening to the entire Bhagavad-Gita from Lord Krishna, Arjuna said:

naṣṭo mohah smṛtir labdhā
tvat-prasādān mayācyuta
sthito 'smi gata-sandehaḥ
kariṣye vacanam tava

'My dear Achyuta (Krishna), by Your grace, all my illusion and confusions are cleared, and I have regained my memory and composure. I am now firm and free from all doubts. I am ready to act according to Your advice' (BG 18.73).

Arjuna who had earlier said, '*dharma-sammūḍha-cetāh*—I am confused about my duty,' is now saying, '*naṣṭo mohah*—All my confusions are cleared.' That is the power of a genuine guide and the Gita wisdom—helping us to find 'clarity' in 'confusion'.

That same Gita wisdom can also act as our guide today in addressing life's perplexities. Although the Gita is an ancient text, its practical message offers solutions to present-day dilemmas.

Practices for Inner Balance

1. *Cultivate the Habit of Seeking Guidance:* When faced with challenges in life, proactively seek guidance from experienced well-wishers or teachers, instead of relying solely on personal judgement.
2. *Practise Humility in Seeking Help:* When the intricacy of a problem is beyond your intelligence to resolve, humbly seek help from a reliable guide with an open mind, without ego or prejudice.
3. *Regularly Evaluate Your Life's Path:* Periodically assess your goals by reflecting on your purpose and decisions, and in case of confusion, seek guidance to realign your path and stay on course.
4. *Balance Emotions and Rationality:* Look for guides who not only empathize with your situation, but also provide rational solutions.
5. *Be a Genuine Well-Wisher:* Strive to help others whenever you can. Balance empathy with practical advice, and sincerely celebrate their successes, free from envy.

6

Withdraw to Win

Navigating Distractions with Wisdom

Sri Kurmam, or Kurma-kshetra, is a village in Srikakulam, a district in the south Indian state of Andhra Pradesh. Sri Kurmam is famous for its temple of Lord Kurma, the gigantic tortoise incarnation of Lord Vishnu. The Bhagavata Purana mentions that Lord Kurma had lifted the gigantic Mandara mountain on His back and gave it the necessary stability to act as a churning rod while the devatas and the demons churned the milk ocean to produce *amrita* or nectar.

In my childhood, we used to live at a place very close to Sri Kurmam, and would often visit the nearby temples. During one of those visits, I saw a tortoise, probably for the first time in my life. It was moving very slowly. Being curious, I went closer. It stopped moving suddenly. I was surprised and paused in my footsteps. A few moments later,

the tortoise popped its head out of its shell and resumed its journey. Once again as I inched forward out of curiosity, the tortoise almost froze like a statue.

The way the tortoise paused its movement was truly a peculiar sight. It would draw its legs and face into its body which was like a small hill, and sit down completely unmoving. After a while, when it thought its path was clear, it slowly unwound itself and set off on the move.

My parents explained to me the nature of a tortoise—with a shell as hard as a rock, the tortoise protects its limbs from dangers and attacks. Whenever it encounters an obstacle, it withdraws its limbs into its shell for protection.

Later, my mother gave me a banana and encouraged me to feed the tortoise. I was a bit hesitant, but still trudged on. Finding a spot beside the tortoise, I sat down with the banana in my hand. I think it noticed me and the banana, and began trusting me. This time, it didn't withdraw its limbs; instead, it slowly crawled towards me and I crawled to it. As we met each other, I took a little piece of the banana and extended my hand to feed it. Soon, it extended its neck, grabbed the piece in its mouth and ate it up. I was thrilled. I fed it the full banana piece by piece, and it feasted and eventually moved on.

The Protective Shield

The behaviour of the tortoise teaches us an important lesson on the art of withdrawal, as Lord Krishna points out in this verse.

yadā saṁharate cāyaṁ
kūrmo 'ṅgānīva sarvaśaḥ
indriyāṇīndriyārthebhyas
tasya prajñā pratiṣṭhitā

'Just as a tortoise withdraws its limbs into the shell, one has to withdraw one's senses from distracting and harmful sense objects. Such a person is perfectly intelligent' (BG 2.58).

To inspire us to practise sense control, Lord Krishna teaches us from the example of a tortoise. Just as a tortoise pulls its limbs inside its shell when things get tough, we can try to withdraw our senses that distract our mind to objects and people that are hurtful.

The tortoise has a natural shield in the form of its hard shell to protect it from all physical dangers. As human beings, we need to build a *protective shield of wisdom* to safeguard our mind from the ever-increasing distractions of this world—be it smartphones, social media or toxic association!

Facing temptations doesn't mean literally facing them; but it means turning your face away from them. Embrace the wisdom of acting like a tortoise.

Those who boast about facing temptations head-on are often the ones most susceptible to giving in.

Sensory Allurements

In the Gita (2.60), Lord Krishna explains,

yatato hy api kaunteya
puruṣasya vipaścitaḥ
indriyāṇi pramāthīni
haranti prasabhaṁ manaḥ

'The senses are so strong and restless that they forcefully drag away the minds of even wise persons who know what is right and what is wrong, even if they are trying hard to control the senses.'

Imagine walking through a bustling market where the vibrant colours catch your eye, the alluring aroma of street food hits your nose, and the chatter of the crowd reaches your ears. As you walk, your senses are inevitably bombarded with various impressions even without you consciously noticing it, and they impact your mind.

Our five senses—eyes, tongue, nose, ears and skin—are like our own personal detectives, always on the lookout for interesting things in the world. They find their objects, namely forms, flavours, scents, sounds and textures, and when they connect with these things, they create various desires, thoughts and emotions in our minds—some good and some not so good. And when we actually bring our senses in contact with their objects, that contact often creates a long-lasting impression on our mind.

Be it the beautiful form of the opposite gender, or a stylish and sophisticated car, or an attractive outfit—the

eyes have a tendency to get attracted to these forms, and that creates a desire in the mind to enjoy them. On the flip side, ugly shapes repel the eyes and mind. Consider the joy derived from tasting a delicious meal. The flavours linger in your mind's memory, prompting a desire to savour it again. On the flip side, an unpleasant taste imprints a not-so-happy memory in your mind, leading you to avoid it in the future. You can extend this to the remaining senses too.

> *In this sensory symphony, each sense collaborates to create a vast tapestry of experiences, which enter the mind as pleasant and unpleasant impressions. Therefore, to avoid being distracted, we need to limit our senses from coming in contact with unfavourable objects.*

Mental Distractions

> *Distractions are not only external but internal too. External distractions are when the senses are allured by the sense objects, but internal distractions are when the mind deliberately starts meditating on them.*

The mind has an incredible power of instigating actions within our bodies. Imagine the *thought* of indulging in a sweet delicacy like a rasagulla. Your mind instantly activates your senses—directing your eyes to locate the sweet shop, your legs to carry you there and your hands to procure the rasagulla. This intricate dance showcases how our thoughts manifest into physical actions,

allowing us to relish life's pleasures. While sometimes they may be natural and essential, at other times, they may be harmful too.

Our minds, like excited kids, sometimes desire more than our bodies can handle. Consider the craving for numerous rasagullas even when our stomachs are already full. Giving in to the mind's demands to overeat takes our bodies on a journey of indigestion, obesity, diabetes and so on.

This trend of the mind can be extended to much more harmful distractions of alcohol, adultery, gambling and what not. After all, the current age provides all ingredients required for one's degradation, isn't it?

Incompatible Connections

Apart from the sensory interactions, our minds are affected by interpersonal interactions as well. Social dealings significantly affect mind-born thoughts and emotions.

Picture a warm reunion with a close friend, evoking feelings of happiness and excitement. Contrast this with a disagreement with a colleague that triggers anger or disappointment. These emotional responses, whether positive or negative, shape our experiences. Sometimes, we find ourselves riding the waves of happiness, and at other times, we navigate through the currents of sadness.

Our minds are like curators, collecting memories from various sensory encounters and interpersonal interactions.

When we deal with people who are toxic in their mentality, exploitative, abusive and selfish, our minds get exhausted and disgusted. Our overall well-being may also get affected. In such cases, we need to take appropriate action instead of just tolerating things silently. And that's what Lord Krishna taught Arjuna, who wanted to avoid war with his own relatives. Lord Krishna told him that whoever is on the path of unrighteousness must be punished, despite the family connections.

But some people are not that cruel, but a bit annoying. They may not cause serious harm like Duryodhana did to the Pandavas, but irritate with their unwitty and unreasonable working styles and speaking ways. Be it a demanding senior at the workplace, a stubborn sibling at home, a possessive friend, a talkative work partner or an overly emotional family member, sometimes we get troubled by such unavoidable connections. Although they are good in various ways, some facet of their personality is incompatible with our personalities or priorities in life.

This is where the art of withdrawal comes to our rescue, and the tortoise acts as our role model.

Following the Tortoise

Whether they are sensory allurements, mental distractions or unreasonable relations, the art of withdrawal can help us more than we think it can. Whenever we are tempted by distractions through external objects or internal recollection, a developed intelligence inspires us to pull

our mind away from temptations. Thus, we win over temptations even before they can attack us.

If we attempt to withdraw our senses from harmful sense objects, and indulge them only in beneficial ones, we can save ourselves from the pain of sensual distractions. This helps maintain a harmonious balance between indulgence and well-being. Since the senses are one type of inlet through which our minds become loaded with unlimited thoughts and cravings, we need to be careful and picky about what we expose our senses to.

Much like the discerning choices we make in nourishing our bodies, a similar mindfulness should govern the nourishment of our minds. Consequently, we must judiciously regulate what we see, consume, hear, smell and touch. This intentional sense control becomes the linchpin for mastering the mind, as encapsulated in the adage, 'Out of sight, out of mind!' Indeed, the governance of the senses paves the way for the governance of the mind.

Sense control leads to mind control.

Coming to the case of incompatible relationships, tolerance, patience and forgiveness are some cool tools to deal with such people. But sometimes, we need to use the tool of withdrawal at least for a while, especially when their natures distract us from our priorities.

For instance, if your nature is to be quiet and soft-spoken, you may feel uncomfortable with a man who is talkative, loud and often gets overexcited. That person may not be inherently bad but is just incompatible with

your mood. Let's say, if he starts an excited conversation in your presence which you are not interested in, you may excuse yourself to go and focus on your work peacefully.

You may not attempt to stop him, but you shouldn't stop your work! He will surely find someone who is compatible with his nature. You may not hate that person, but for you to focus on your priorities, you need to maintain a respectful distance from that person, and respect him from a distance, instead of being disrespectful to him by coming close.

We need to respect everyone, but we cannot be close to everyone.

If coming close to certain people makes us annoyed, disrespectful and fills our mind with negativity, distancing ourselves would be a better option.

Milk is good and nourishing food, and so is a lemon. But you know what happens when we mix the two. So, we're better off keeping them separate. The same is exactly the case with people. Respectful distance avoids unnecessary friction between people. Drawing reasonable boundaries, giving space to people and taking the space that you need keeps relationships dignified and sensible.

Maintain a respectful distance from incompatible people, and respect them from a distance.

These sensual and internal personal interactions oftentimes distract our mind from what truly matters to us.

Practices for Inner Balance

1. *Practise the Art of Withdrawal:* Emulate the behaviour of the tortoise by withdrawing your senses from distracting and harmful sense objects, instead of confronting them.
2. *Sharpen Your Intellect:* Build a protective shield of wisdom to safeguard your mind from external distractions such as smartphones, social media and toxic associations.
3. *Limit Sensory Interactions:* Regulate your senses and their interactions with the external world, to avoid distractions—desires, thoughts and emotions—that can divert your focus.
4. *Evaluate Interpersonal Connections:* Maintain a respectful distance from people whose behaviours are incompatible with your values and priorities. Draw reasonable boundaries, give and take space, and avoid unnecessary friction to maintain dignified and sensible relationships.

7

Mindfulness in a Digital Age

Finding Peace Amidst Distractions

Once, I saw a little boy, hardly a year old, sitting on his mother's lap, as she busied herself in a conversation with her friend. The boy was joyful and smiling. Every now and then, he tried to get out of his mother's lap, or extend his hands and touch the objects around him.

When he touched a fruit, the mom smiled and allowed him to play with it. In a few moments, he threw the fruit, and it rolled on the ground. He crawled behind it for a few baby steps, but eventually gave up the chase. Then, he found a knife nearby and picked it up. His mother immediately came over, took it away and put him back on her lap. He was disappointed and flapped his hands and legs for freedom. So his mother offered a toy to pacify him, and he played with it for a while. Then, he left the toy, took his mother's handbag and tried to put its belt into his

mouth. His mother gently pulled it away as she continued to converse. She also put the toy back in her son's hands. And this continued to happen . . .

Whenever the child touched something soft and harmless, the mother would allow him to do so, but when he reached out for something harmful, his mother immediately took it away and brought him back to her lap. Even when the baby cried, the mom comforted him and kept him on her lap. And this is how we need to control our curious, restless, fickle and unsteady minds. Interesting, isn't it?

Getting distracted is natural, but remaining distracted is harmful.

The Kid Called Mind

The mind is like an innocent kid, lively and curious. To keep the mind calm and composed amidst the chaotic distractions of this world is a great challenge. The mind is also a storehouse of all kinds of thoughts, desires, emotions and feelings. Some of them positive, while others are negative. The mind collects all these impressions through the senses and interactions with people around us.

The mind is always eager to explore everything, but it doesn't know what's right or wrong, good or bad. That's where our intelligence comes in, just like a mom guiding her child. Intelligence keeps a watchful eye on the mind's activities, just like a vigilant mother, and practises bringing the mind's focus back to the task at hand. But our intelligence will function in this way only when it has

been trained and sharpened. Now, the question is: *Are we prepared to do so?*

What Is Attentiveness?

In this world, it is not possible to remain undistracted. But a wise person is the one who consciously brings his mind back whenever it gets distracted. This concept finds resonance in the teachings of the Bhagavad-Gita (6.26).

yato yato niścalati
manaś cañcalam asthiram
tatas tato niyamyaitad
ātmany eva vaśam nayet

'From wherever the restless mind wanders, one must withdraw it and bring it back under one's control.'

> *The consistent attempt to bring the distracted mind back and make it focus on the task at hand is called attentiveness.*

We've all witnessed how playful children run away from their mothers, to explore things around them. And then we've seen how their anxious mothers chase after them to prevent any kind of accident or mishap. Similarly, our mind runs away towards different objects and places, even if they are not necessary or relevant. If we allow our mind to indulge in thoughts, desires and feelings that are harmful or counterproductive, we risk drifting aimlessly. But that doesn't mean we should hate our mind. We need to tame and calm our mind like mothers do.

uddhared ātmanātmānaṁ
nātmānam avasādayet
ātmaiva hy ātmano bandhur
ātmaiva ripur ātmanaḥ
bandhur ātmātmanas tasya
yenātmaivātmanā jitaḥ
anātmanas tu śatrutve
vartetātmaiva śatru-vat

Lord Krishna says, 'If you can regulate the mind's distractions, it acts like your friend, but if you leave it uncontrolled, it becomes your worst enemy. Elevate yourself by the power of your mind, and do not degrade yourself. The mind can work both like a friend and an enemy. For those who regulate the mind, it is their best friend. For those who have failed to do so, the mind works like the worst enemy' (BG 6.5–6).

But hold on . . . is this as easy as it appears to be?

A Piece of Cake?

You may think, 'It's easier said than done! Is pulling the mind back always possible?' Concentrating the mind on one activity is a great challenge, especially in this digital age, amidst smartphones, social media and sensory distractions.

Even the mighty warrior Arjuna found it difficult. 'My dear Krishna, the mind is restless, turbulent, obstinate and very strong. I think controlling the mind is more difficult than controlling the wind,' Arjuna said, in great discomfort.

Being an expert and experienced warrior, Arjuna had the knowledge of several *mantras* with which he would empower his arrows with magical powers. In battle, he could use a wind-weapon, water-weapon, fire-weapon and so on. Just by chanting a hymn, he could invoke wind or fire in his arrow and direct it to destroy his enemies in the battle. Thus, Arjuna found it easier to control the wind but not the mind.

> *We can't underestimate the extent of the mind's distractions, and can never be overconfident about controlling it.*

Lord Krishna didn't dismiss Arjuna's concern, rather He acknowledged it, and provided an actionable solution for mind control. When someone expresses their difficulty, we need to be sensitive to their situation and try to assist them with the best possible solution, instead of suppressing or oppressing their expressions. Even if we can't really present a solution, simply hearing out their problem empathetically can calm their minds to some extent.

Two Keys to Tame the Mind

Lord Krishna responded to Arjuna's concern by presenting two effective tips to regulate the mind's distractions. He said:

asaṃśayam mahā-bāho
mano durnigraham calam
abhyāsena tu kaunteya
vairāgyeṇa ca gṛhyate

'O mighty-armed Arjuna, it is undoubtedly very difficult to regulate the restless mind, but it is possible by (1) Practice (*abhyāsa*) and (2) Detachment (*vairagya*).'

Lord Krishna also describes the hierarchy of the body's elements, and says, 'The senses are inferior to the mind, and the intelligence is superior to the mind.' Because the mind is positioned between intelligence and the senses, we can regulate the mind from both sides by (1) Sense Control, and (2) Sharp Intelligence.

Combining the above two pairs of keys, we can tame our mind with the following two actionable practices, the first external and the second, internal:

1. Practise Sense Control
2. Cultivate Detachment with Intelligence

1. *Practise Sense Control:* The senses act as the entry points through which the mind receives various impressions. Therefore, by regulating the senses from overindulging in the sense objects, we eventually bring the mind under control. By doing so, we restrict unnecessary inputs to the mind, and thus regulate the mind's distractions. This is the external way to tame the mind. As mentioned before: 'Out of sight, out of mind.'
2. *Cultivate Detachment through Intelligence:* Although keeping distractions physically out of sight is a good way to control the mind, our inner thoughts can distract us too. With sharp intelligence,

we should dismiss such thoughts, and cultivate detachment from things that are unfavourable for our well-being. Knowing the transient nature of the pleasures of this world helps us be detached from them. We can sharpen our intelligence by doing two things: (1) reading wisdom texts like the Gita and (2) learning from experienced people.

The mind can be brought from distraction to concentration, by using scriptural intelligence to analyse its thoughts and align them with values.

Thus, by restricting the senses externally and sharpening the intelligence internally, we can tame our unsteady mind and make it our greatest friend.

When a lamp in a windy place wavers, we protect its flame by enclosing it with our hands. Similarly, we need to protect the flame of our minds from the wind of distractions with the hands of our intelligence.

Practices for Inner Balance

1. *Practise Sense Control*: Identify the sources of distraction, such as social media, notifications or other sensory inputs, and limit access to them by creating specific time blocks for focused work or study.
2. *Cultivate Detachment through Intelligence*: Regularly reflect on your thoughts and assess whether they align with your values and goals. Practise dismissing negative or counterproductive thoughts and focus on cultivating a sense of detachment from things that hinder your well-being.
3. *Read Wisdom Texts*: Dedicate time daily or weekly to read wisdom texts that can provide insights on mindfulness and focus. Take notes and reflect on how the teachings can be applied to your own life.
4. *Learn from Experienced People*: Learn from seasoned people, either in person or through books, podcasts or online platforms, and gather practical tips on how they have managed to control distractions and stay focused.
5. *Set Clear Boundaries*: Define specific periods for work or study, and communicate these boundaries to others. Create a conducive environment by minimizing potential distractions during these focused periods.

8

Immersed Minds

Unleashing Productivity through Determination

In the sacred confines of our temple, I once entered the worship room for my service of cleansing the vessels. First, I had to clean a good lot of copper cups, traditionally known as *acamana patras*, integral in the worship of the deities in temples.

Our general practice is to immerse copper vessels in tamarind water where copper's encounter with tamarind swiftly restores its brilliance. We had a big steel vessel that held a solution of tamarind water, where all the small copper cups were submerged by the preceding volunteer.

Upon commencing my service, I discovered one copper cup afloat in the tamarind water, not fully immersed. As I lifted it, I found the portion of the cup beneath the water revealed a pristine, bright pink shine,

but the remaining portion was blackish. I tried to clean it with a scrubber and soap, but it wasn't that fruitful.

I kept the cup back in the tamarind water, this time fully submerging it. I then washed the remaining vessels, and after some time, took the cup out and found it shining. This incident made me reflect on a profound lesson from the Bhagavad-Gita:

> *True excellence arises when the mind is fully immersed in the task at hand.*

Recalling the incident, I recognized the significance of immersion. Just as the half-immersed cup was only partially clean, a distracted mind can only yield incomplete results. In contrast, a fully absorbed mind, much like the completely immersed copper cups, assimilates knowledge and produces optimal outcomes.

> *Cultivate absorption in your endeavours to unlock the depths of productivity.*

The Power of Determination

Immersing our mind and intelligence in the task at hand enhances productivity and guarantees a more fulfilling outcome. On the contrary, succumbing to distractions and diverting our mind to unproductive things hampers the attainment of our goals.

In this regard, Lord Krishna says in the Bhagavad-Gita (2.41) that successful people are those who have one pointed focus on their goals, while unsuccessful people get distracted by many things.

vyavasāyātmikā buddhir
ekeha kuru-nandana
bahu-śākhā hy anantāś ca
buddhayo 'vyavasāyinām

'Those who are determined to attain their goals, fully focus on the necessary means to attain the goal, without getting diverted towards irrelevant things. But the intelligence of those who are not determined is diverted towards so many things, and they ultimately cannot reach their goals.'

Arjuna, the foremost student of the Bhagavad-Gita, stands as a paragon of focus and determination. As a student of his military teacher, Drona, Arjuna exhibited full immersion in his learning, and thus became his teacher's favourite student. His unyielding commitment serves as a beacon, underscoring the significance of these attributes in the pursuit of our objectives in life.

Once, Drona, the guru of the Pandavas, wanted to test his students. He tied a wooden bird to the top of a tree and asked each prince to prepare to shoot it down. As they aimed at the bird with their arrows, Drona asked them to describe what they saw. Most of the princes broadly depicted what they saw—their teachers, their colleagues, the tree, the sky, the garden, the wooden bird on the branch, and so on. Drona then asked Arjuna. Arjuna replied, 'I see only the bird's eye.'

Impressed, Drona told his students, 'A focused warrior sees only his target, and nothing else.'

Arjuna's singular focus and determination enabled him to achieve mastery in archery. Such is the focus required to

attain our purposes, whether material or spiritual, despite a plethora of allurements and distractions in this world.

> *Success in any endeavour is directly proportional to the depth of our determination and focus.*

Can we develop determination similar to Arjuna's? Absolutely. But the most important key to develop determination is discernment.

Discernment Aids Determination

The mind houses multiple desires that are developed when our senses interact with sense objects and people. But all the desires of the mind are not beneficial, some are even harmful. Although the mind instigates us to fulfil all its desires, we need to equip our intelligence with the ability to discriminate between the beneficial and the harmful. The ancient texts give us the key to attain the goals: '*anukulasya sankalpam pratikulasya varjanam*—Accept the favourable and abandon the unfavourable.'

> *Possessing right discrimination between the good and the bad, the right and the wrong, the auspicious and the inauspicious, empowers our decision-making. Discrimination ensures that our choices align with the overarching purpose of our lives.*

Intelligent discrimination of the mind's desires and working on beneficial desires with determination help us attain our life's purposes. Such a refined and intelligent choice of things to do and well-thought-out execution

plans keep our life's course productive. Thus, we can safeguard ourselves from potential distractions. Building a shield against diversions ensures a steadfast journey towards our meaningful objectives.

True determination based on such discernment is not deterred by obstacles; instead, challenges become stepping stones to a stronger resolve. It is a mindset that defies demotivation, emphasizing the need to persist in the face of adversity.

Discernment also helps us use our time judiciously. Time, a precious resource, demands thoughtful utilization. When we value time and acknowledge that we have limited time in life, we can become determined to focus on our goals, by fully immersing ourselves in the means to attain those goals. Such immersion elevates productivity and enhances the quality of our endeavours through effective time management.

Make your life fulfilling with meaningful desires and determined endeavours.

So, are 'discernment in desires' and 'determination in endeavours' the only parameters to attain worthy goals in life? Here is an answer that makes the discussion more complete.

The Triad of Attainment

Having a worthy and well-thought-out desire is great, but it must be followed by determined endeavour. Sincere efforts are great but they must be sanctioned by

higher powers. Therefore, prayer becomes a necessary part of life's journey to attain anything.

Desire, endeavour and prayer form the trinity of tools to attain worthy goals.

Thoughtful desire and determined action, coupled with sincere prayer, constitute a formidable approach. However, the ultimate sanction lies in the Lord's mercy. Our desires must align with values and efforts must be sincere and consistent, but they must be approved, blessed and sanctioned by the Almighty Lord as well. So, we need to offer prayers to the Lord before and during the execution of any plans and be detached from the results.

We should do our best and leave the rest to divine intervention.

Aligning our mind and intellect with devotional practices of meditation and prayers brings clarity, purpose and an unwavering commitment to our ultimate goal.

Through discrimination in desire, determination in endeavour, and devotion in prayer, we pave the way for goal attainment. The synergy of these elements propels us towards success, making our journey purposeful and enriching. Such achievements are materially useful and spiritually meaningful.

Sometimes, absorption in an activity without diversions could lead to overly passionate work that may have a toll on our physical health and may also increase mental stress, lead to relationship disruptions among other things. So how can we deal with all of that and more? That only the next chapter can reveal.

Practices for Inner Balance

1. *Practise Immersion in Tasks:* Stay fully present in your tasks by eliminating distractions, creating a focused workspace and setting specific time blocks for undisturbed work.
2. *Cultivate Determination:* Set clear goals, break them into manageable chunks, create a plan with milestones and consistently work towards your objectives, displaying resilience in overcoming obstacles.
3. *Develop Discernment:* Distinguish between beneficial and harmful desires, and prioritize tasks that contribute positively to your life.
4. *Manage Your Time Wisely:* Use your time judiciously by aligning tasks with goals. Create a daily schedule that balances your work, personal life and relaxation. Prioritize tasks based on importance and urgency.
5. *Incorporate Prayer and Devotion:* Integrate prayer and devotional practices for spiritual clarity. Dedicate time for meditation, aligning goals with higher values, seeking guidance and cultivating gratitude.

Practices for (Inner) Balance

9

Boundaries That Empower

Finding Freedom in a Regulated Existence

'You don't have to be passionate to be productive.' This was an inference I made from a discourse given by a senior monk in the ashram. 'What do you expect to achieve when you lack passion?' someone might question. To me this question sounds both logical and practical. This is because I have witnessed the lives of several successful individuals unfold before me. The role of passion in their lives had been almost like that of hot peppers in a dish—bringing in a punch of flavour and energy. But hadn't the monk spoken about diluting our passion? Well, what he was indicating in essence was *rajo-guna*, a word that Lord Krishna uses in the Gita, a designation for the mode of passion.

Many times, the word 'passion' is used in a positive sense to promote determination and focus. However, the monk highlighted the flipside of passion—which makes

one overly ambitious and restless. Indeed, he had been prompting us to reflect on the balance needed for true productivity and spiritual well-being.

But there is more to *rajo-guna* and the way things work in this world. To get a broader understanding of the dynamics of universal functioning, let's explore Lord Krishna's teachings in the Gita.

The Trilateral Set-up

There are three natural forces in this world that impel human beings to act in various ways, and thus experience happiness, distress, stress and so on. These forces affect how we think and behave, leading to good or not-so-good outcomes. In the Bhagavad-Gita (14.5), Lord Krishna describes these forces, called *gunas* or the modes of nature: *Sattva, Rajas* and *Tamas.*

sattvam rajas tama iti
guṇāḥ prakṛti-sambhavāḥ
nibadhnanti mahā-bāho
dehe dehinam avyayam

'Nature consists of three gunas or modes: *Sattva* (goodness), *Rajas* (passion) and *Tamas* (ignorance). The living being who comes in contact with nature, becomes bound by these modes.'

1. *Sattva-guna (Goodness)*: *Sattva* is characterized by wisdom and clarity, and it enables effective decision-making. It represents goodness, wisdom

and happiness. The minds and intelligence of those who are in *sattva* are bright like the light of the sun and the moon. Such people can see things clearly and understand them better.

2. *Rajo-guna (Passion)*: *Rajas* is characterized by strong desire, restlessness, impatience and intense attachment. It makes us want things and gives us the energy to chase our desires. An element of *rajas* is certainly required for all creative tasks. Those who are strongly influenced by *rajas* are very ambitious, super-busy, hyperactive, work hard for their achievements and take great pride in their accomplishments.
3. *Tamo-guna (Ignorance)*: *Tamas* is characterized by ignorance and laziness, which often results in a lack of self-preservation. It represents darkness and bewilderment. The minds of those who are influenced by *tamas* are confused, weak and ignorant of their own welfare. They perform deeds without knowledge and wisdom, and even harm themselves.

People predominantly influenced by *sattva* can face the chaos of life with maturity, even transforming negative stress into a catalyst for personal growth. Those under the sway of *rajas* may struggle or sometimes succeed with great effort in the face of challenges. Those influenced by *tamas* are mostly at a disadvantage, living in confusion and bewilderment.

The Art of Balancing Passion and Goodness

It is evident that *sattva* is the best, *tamas* is the worst and *rajas* is in between. The influence of three forces is spread all over the world. They affect the thoughts and actions of almost everyone. By understanding their functions, we can work towards having more *sattva* in our lives and reducing the impact of *rajas* and *tamas*. This helps us become better and happier individuals. It aligns with the idea of striving for a more harmonious and balanced existence, as taught in the Bhagavad-Gita.

> *To effectively cope with life's chaos, we must transcend the influences of rajas and tamas and cultivate sattva.*

The Bhagavad-Gita wisely counsels us on the delicate balance required in the pursuit of our goals. While determination is crucial, an excess of ambition and passion may lead to a fervour that, if unchecked, disrupts the equilibrium of our lives.

Absorbing ourselves in focused, undistracted work is commendable, but it should not come at the cost of health and mental well-being or lead to strained relationships. Genuine success transcends mere professional achievements; it necessitates a thoughtful reflection on life's true purpose and a deliberate alignment of priorities to foster a holistic and enduring sense of accomplishment.

We must ensure that we don't foster impatience (symptom of *rajas*) in the garb of determination (symptom of *sattva*). Also, patience (symptom of *sattva*) should not

breed complacency (symptom of *tamas*). Striking a delicate balance between determination and patience ensures sustained progress without stagnation in our life's journey.

Determination ≠ Impatience
Patience ≠ Complacency

Oftentimes, we are biased towards achievements, name, fame, figures, influence, accomplishments and distinction, and neglect certain basic and core needs of life—health, peace of mind and relationships.

In a world driven by external markers of success like wealth, fame and status, one may lose sight of what truly matters, and even basic bodily necessities. Therefore, Lord Krishna urges us in the Bhagavad-Gita not to be overly ambitious, but learn the art of regulating and balancing the four basic aspects of life:

yuktāhāra-vihārasya
yukta-ceṣṭasya karmasu
yukta-svapnāvabodhasya
yogo bhavati duhkha-hā

'One who is regulated in one's habits of eating, sleeping, recreation and work can avoid difficulties in life' (BG 16.7).

Having balance in sleeping, eating, recreation and work is essential for maintaining our overall well-being. Apart from these, the real balance in life comes from adding spiritual practices into your routine. Here's how you can do it.

1. Balanced Eating

A lifestyle of sustained energy and overall well-being requires a balanced diet. Mindful eating, where we savour each bite and attune ourselves to hunger and fullness cues, fosters a harmonious connection between the body and nourishment. It is recommended that we chew deliberately, not just for taste, but for optimal digestion.

To maintain consistent energy throughout the day, we need to avoid the pitfalls of skipping meals, recognizing that such lapses can disrupt the symphony of our daily activities. Equally, overindulgence, besides inducing physical discomfort, can cast a shadow on our mental clarity.

> *Undereating makes us weak, and overeating makes us lazy.*

It's better to opt for clean, home-made meals, recognizing the inherent value not just in nutritional content but in the familial care infused within each dish.

> *Before each meal, let us thank the Lord, the ultimate provider of our meals. This cultivates a deeper sense of connection with the Lord amidst our daily hustle.*

In this context, Lord Krishna also talks about three types of foods that we eat, according to the three modes (BG 17.8–10).

1. *Sattvic Foods*: *Sattvic* foods are pure, clean, juicy and wholesome. They increase your lifespan, purity, strength, health, happiness and satisfaction. They promote clarity, focus and overall well-being. Include a variety of fruits, vegetables, whole grains and nuts in your meals. These foods are not only nutritious but also help in maintaining sustained energy levels. They align with the principle of *sattva* or purity, fostering a calm and focused mind.
2. *Rajasic Foods*: *Rajasic* foods are those that include spicy or stimulating elements. They are excessively bitter, sour, salty, hot, pungent, dry and burning. They may give momentary excitement but could cause health troubles over the long run. While some level of energy is essential, avoid excessive consumption of carbonated beverages and spicy snacks. These foods, if consumed in excess, can lead to energy crashes and disrupt sleep. Moderation is key, aligning with the concept of *rajas* or passion. It's important to balance the energizing aspects with a focus on overall health.
3. *Tamasic Foods*: *Tamasic* foods are those that are stale, tasteless, bad-smelling, processed, decomposed and consisting of remnants of untouchable things. Non-veg food is one example. These foods have a dulling effect on the mind. Even overeating falls into this category, leading to sleepiness, tiredness and potential health issues like obesity and indigestion. This aligns with the principle of *tamas*

or inertia, cautioning against choices that can dull the body and mind.

2. **Balanced Snooze Time**
   In our quest for balanced life, quality sleep plays a key role in our physical and mental health. Establishing a consistent sleep schedule, ideally aligning with the natural rhythms of sunset and sunrise, sets the stage for a transformative shift in our overall well-being.

   Just as overeating and undereating are discouraged, oversleeping and undersleeping are also not recommended. Sleep helps rejuvenate the body and refreshes the mind. If our body doesn't get sufficient rest, we can't work, think or interact with people efficiently. And if we sleep more than required, that makes us lazy and ignorant.

   > *Expressing gratitude to the Lord before sleeping and upon waking adds a layer of spiritual connection to our rest, making this nightly routine more than just a physical necessity but a sacred bridge to the divine within our daily lives.*

3. **Balanced Work**
   In our pursuit of meaningful work and a fulfilling life, it is recommended that we cultivate effective time management and realistic goal-setting. Big chunks of work can be overwhelming, and so,

breaking down larger tasks into manageable chunks works better. We can prioritize tasks based on their importance and timelines.

To guard against burnout, it is beneficial to take breaks during work for mental rejuvenation and avoid being overwhelmed.

A healthy work-life balance involves setting clear boundaries and allocating time for professional responsibilities, personal life and spiritual practices of meditation and prayer. Further, offering the results of work for the service of the Lord makes the whole work experience truly fulfilling. My beloved Guru Radhanath Swami often advises spiritual seekers who are working for their livelihood in this way: 'Earn with integrity, and spend with compassion.'

> *True productivity arises not solely from an overly ambitious and restless work schedule but from the wisdom of a balanced lifestyle.*

4. Balanced Play

Regular breaks during work sessions, engaged in activities we enjoy, are not mere leisurely pursuits; they are essential for stress relief and mental well-being. It is recommended that we recognize the significance of recreation as more than just a pause; it is a deliberate reset, a conscious recharging of creative energies.

Striking a balance between productive work and enjoyable downtime involves a mindful approach to our routines. It is recommended that we acknowledge the importance of pauses in the symphony of our lives, crafting moments that resonate with joy and purpose.

> *In the intricate dance between productivity and relaxation, it is beneficial to carve out spaces for rejuvenation.*

In summary, balancing sleeping, eating, working and recreation involves creating routines that prioritize self-care, setting realistic goals and recognizing the importance of both productivity and relaxation. By paying attention to these aspects, you can enhance your overall health and well-being, leading to improved academic performance and a more enjoyable experience.

Practices for Inner Balance

1. *Cultivating Sattva:* Strive to cultivate the qualities of goodness, and gradually rise above the influence of *rajas* and *tamas*.
2. *Mindful Eating:* Savour each bite and prioritize a balanced diet with *sattvic* foods for sustained energy and a harmonious connection between body and nourishment.
3. *Quality Sleep:* Maintain a consistent sleep schedule, express gratitude before bedtime and recognize the rejuvenating role of sleep for physical and mental well-being.
4. *Effective Work-Life Balance:* Enhance productivity with effective time management, breaks for mental rejuvenation and a healthy work-life balance aligned with a sense of purpose.
5. *Recreation for Stress Relief:* Acknowledge recreation as a deliberate reset for creative energies, and engage in enjoyable activities during breaks for stress relief and mental well-being.
6. *Balanced Spiritual Practices:* Integrate spiritual practices for overall well-being, cultivating determination without impatience, patience without complacency, and maintaining balance across achievements, health, peace of mind and relationships.

10

The Grey Area of Desire

Contemporary Insights on Love, Lust and Everything in Between

'What is the difference between love and lust?' I wondered as a young boy.

In those days, many movies depicted love primarily as romance between a young man and woman. But deep within my intellect, there was an understanding that love is universal and exists amongst family members, friends, siblings and even animals. Also, the thought that love has forms other than that which exists between young boys and girls made much sense to me. The term 'love' in its truest sense meant much more than an amorous exchange. This was the realization I had.

The way today's society overly glamorizes infatuation or 'lust in the name of love' contributes to our understanding of love. Therefore, in this world, physical

attraction towards the beauty of the opposite gender has been defined as the cornerstone of love. Sometimes, the mind's desire for physical pleasures is also sugarcoated with the term 'love'! Now let's explore the difference between love and lust.

My real understanding of the fundamental difference between lust (*kāma*) and love (*prema*) became profound when I took to the spiritual path, and especially when I heard a scriptural statement that meant:

> *'Lust is a selfish desire to enjoy oneself, especially on a sensual platform, and love is a selfless desire to please the beloved.'* (Source: *Sri Caitanya Caritamrita)*

The Spectrum of Lust

Lust is generally referred to as a strong inclination for sense enjoyment; but lust also refers to a passionate desire to enjoy anything, including material possessions, fame, position, status, power and so on. When desires become insatiable and uncontrollable, that's one of the signs of lust coming into play. These desires may extend beyond basic needs, creating a constant craving for more, which can be a source of inner turmoil. An inability to control one's thoughts and actions, particularly in the face of tempting situations, indicates the influence of lust. This lack of restraint can lead to impulsive decisions with long-term consequences.

Kāma is the Sanskrit word that encompasses the multiple shades and the entire spectrum of desire or lust. Lord Krishna describes in the Bhagavad-Gita that the cause

of lust is bad association (*sangāt sañjāyate kāmah,* 2.62). Our desires and aspirations are shaped according to the company we keep.

Close friendship with lusty people makes us lusty. In contrast to this, being in proximity with self-controlled and cultured people keeps us sane and composed. Therefore, the Bhagavad-Gita and all wisdom texts recommend that we stay away from lust-inducing associations and embrace spiritually minded people who disseminate and teach us the path of loving God and His children.

Lust creates chaos in our lives, while love calms our hearts.

While lust can mean desire in general and sensual desires specifically, lust is actually a *misdirected desire*. Every living being's original desire is to love God, but as soon as one starts identifying with the body, one starts craving for bodily desires and enters into the arena of misdirected desires.

Desire is inherently not bad or harmful, if channelized in the proper direction, but misdirected desires are certainly harmful for one's material or spiritual well-being. Furthermore, they cause great damage to others as well. A victim of lust becomes a culprit in the lives of others who thus become victims.

Victims of lust create many victims of their lust.

Lust often skews priorities, causing people to prioritize immediate gratification over long-term well-being. When

lust is at play, ethical and moral considerations take a back seat, not to speak of spiritual principles.

Is Desire Bad?

Lust is a natural instinct of any average individual. While in infancy or early childhood, this form of lust is not manifest, it becomes more apparent with age and development of the bodily senses. Not only human beings, even animals and birds have this inclination.

But the fundamental difference between humans and non-humans in expressing their sensual desire is *culture*. Human beings are expected to be more dignified, refined, regulated and modest in expressing their desires for enjoyment. The simple reason for this is that human beings have a greater purpose in life.

And what exactly is that greater purpose? Now give this a thought. If animals eat, sleep, mate and defend themselves, and humans mirror their behaviour, then what would really distinguish us from them? Being equipped with an intelligence superior to that of animals, humans should strive to utilize their energy for a spiritual purpose. Ultimately, being spiritual in nature, our eternal happiness lies not in bodily pleasures, but in an unending spiritual relationship with God, and on that basis, loving other children of God.

Our ultimate happiness lies in serving God.

Being humans, we should regulate our desires within the virtuous system of marriage and channelize them for the

noble cause of giving birth to responsible individuals. That would actually be a service to society and the Lord. Lord Krishna Himself confirms in the Bhagavad-Gita: '*dharma aviruddho bhūteshu kāmo asmi*—I am sex life which is not contrary to virtuous principles' (7.11). Many noble souls in the past have responsibly begot wonderful children and trained them in virtues, values and culture; thus contributing to society apart from attaining personal happiness.

One who is under the sway of uncontrolled desires suffers from a disrupted value system, and eventually loses discrimination and even the hesitation to harm others. Such a person is deprived of physical, mental and spiritual balance, and gives up morality and basic human dignity.

Those who desire freedom for their lust are bound by that very lust.

The Inner Enemy

Sometimes, we may consider people as enemies while at other times, people may consider us as their enemies. But the truth is that everyone has a common enemy: lust. Some people fight for lust, instead of fighting lust. Even the worst enemy in our life can pursue us only till death. But lust is one such antagonist that pursues us life after life.

The most dangerous enemy is the one we can't see.

Ravana, the demon king, was blinded by lust for Mother Sita, which made him deaf to the advice of his

well-wishing brother, Vibhishana. Although he was a great warrior who conquered many heroes, he was victimized by lust. This brought about his ruination and the destruction of his race.

Unregulated desires induce insensitivity, shamelessness, perversion and exploitative tendencies in people who thus become worse than brutal beasts. Lust robs us of our common sense and discernment. Therefore, in the Gita, Lord Krishna describes lust as the all-devouring sinful enemy of the soul.

Sometimes, the best way to deal with lust is to starve it.

Now, let's do a deep-dive into the progressive stages of lust.

Ten Stages of Lust

There are ten stages in which lust attacks and causes degradation of an individual. Here they are.

1. *Cakshū-rāga:* Attraction through the eyes
2. *Cittāsanga:* Intense attachment in the mind
3. *Sankalpa:* Determination to attain the object of lust
4. *Nidrā-ccheda:* Loss of sleep
5. *Tanutā:* Becoming emaciated
6. *Vishaya-nivritti:* Disinterest in other things
7. *Trapā-nasa:* Shamelessness
8. *Unmāda:* Madness
9. *Mūrcchā:* Fainting
10. *Mriti:* Death

Unfortunately, the modern-day ambience at many places presents several lust-inducing visuals. When the eyes are glued to those visuals, the mind becomes blinded with lust. The more the eyes indulge in obscene visuals, the more the mind gets locked in an insane embrace of lust. That attachment and infatuation of the mind makes one determined to enjoy the object of one's lust, not acknowledging the terrible consequences. The mental fascination drives one through the remaining stages of loss of sleep, shamelessness, madness and so on. The origin of this cyclical development of lust is the deliberate indulgence of the eyes in vulgarity.

When the eyes indulge in obscene visuals, the mind becomes obsessed with lust.

Even when the eyes do not come in contact with lust-inducing sense objects, the mind that was infatuated with lust due to previous sensual impressions induces the eyes to search for obscenity even when it is not present. And this leads people into a never-ending chaos in their lives and others' as well.

But a question that may come up is: 'Can sense pleasures relieve one from the stress and exhaustion caused by life's challenges?'

Well, let's find out.

Sense Pleasures a Stress Buster?

During my childhood, I once got a rash on my hand. This caused an unbearable itching sensation. This was probably

the result of an allergy or infection, but my childhood innocence had kept me oblivious to it. I naturally started scratching my hand with my fingernails to relieve myself of the itch. The moment I stopped scratching, I felt the prickliness increase. I scratched even more, this time with greater vigour, but I still kept feeling itchier. The more I scratched, the more did the urge to scratch inflate. Despite my skin getting reddish and puffy, my urge to scratch refused to abate. I didn't realize that my infection was increasing.

Before I could figure it out, I inadvertently used the same fingernails to scratch my neck, head, legs, etc., and the infection spread to those parts as well. Eventually, I found myself scratching all over my body, which then became reddish and puffy at various places. Finally, I ran to my mother to inform her about my situation. She was worried, and with the assistance of my grandmother, she applied some ointment, gave me some medicine and strictly told me:

'Do not scratch!!!'

Because my scratching inflamed my urge to scratch, I was told not to. Something similar is the case with lust. The more we indulge in sensual pleasures, the more we hanker for them, till they transform into an undoable addiction.

Sometimes, people turn into advocates of sense pleasures, proclaiming them to be the source of respite from life's miseries. They consider that all forms of sensual pleasures are mind-calming exercises.

But the basic problem with such indulgences is the *addiction* they bring along—both mental and physical. Just as scratching wasn't the treatment for my infection but a means to aggravate it, similarly, unrestricted sensual indulgences don't serve as stress-busters but peace-busters. Once we get addicted to forbidden pleasures, we end up wasting our valuable time and energy, alienating ourselves from others in seeking secret sensual pleasures. Resultantly, we may even compromise on our dignity and morality. Ultimately, by roaming on the platform of bodily pleasures, we deprive ourselves of a higher and unending spiritual pleasure.

But in contrast to this saga of sensual indulgence, there are better prospects in life for our pursuits for pleasure. And what exactly are they?

Healthy Pursuits for Pleasure

While the world exalts satisfying lusty desires as a great source of pleasure, the self-evident life experiences reveal that there are other, richer sources of pleasure.

Remember a moment in your life when you craved for something intensely and eventually got it, but really didn't experience the happiness that you had actually expected.

The world's promises of pleasure are far from reality.

We need to strive to regulate sensual urges and divert human energy and time towards more productive activities, and grow in our personal, professional and spiritual lives effectively.

Lust induces a selfish 'enjoy or exploit' mentality whenever we come in contact with beauty. But by practising a spiritual life, we can give up this selfish mentality to exploit the beauty of this world, and learn to develop a selfless mentality to utilize the objects of this world in the service of its creator, the Supreme Almighty Lord.

Beauty should inspire us to appreciate the creator of the beauty, and by doing so, we will be spiritually elevated. A spiritual seeker realizes the dexterity of the creator God in manifesting that beauty.

> *Every phenomenon, object, situation and person in this world provides opportunities to uplift our spirit if only we have the right kind of outlook. Thus, a life journey devoid of lust leads to spiritual elevation instead of material degradation.*

And how exactly can we attain such a consciousness and perspective? By associating with wise people and reading wisdom texts like the Bhagavad-Gita, we are introduced to greater sources of enduring pleasure in contrast to fleeting material pleasures.

It so happened that I once felt mentally perturbed due to an unfulfilled expectation. With such an unsettled mindset, I headed to the temple of Lord Krishna. As I observed His beautifully decorated form from His toes to His head, with the peacock feather, turban, flute in His hands and His threefold bending form in a shining outfit, my mind automatically switched gears and calmed down. The power of spiritual beauty lies in pacifying the mind

with a desire to seek shelter, while material beauty often agitates it with a desire to enjoy pleasure.

> *Material beauty agitates the mind, spiritual beauty satisfies the mind.*

Regulate Lust and Revive Love

Lust steals away our consciousness just as weeds suck away the nutrients in a field depriving the main crop from its nourishment. To regulate lust, Lord Krishna gives us some keys in the Gita:

1. *Sense Control:* By keeping safe distance from lust-inducing visuals and sense objects, we can tolerate the temptations of the senses, and hence, terminating the tribulations of lust becomes easy.
2. *Intellectual Control:* Knowledge is a potent tool in overcoming the illusions created by lust and getting detached. However beautiful the bodies of people are, they are ultimately bags of flesh, blood, bones, nerves, urine and stool, just covered by a layer of skin. Showing off one's skin, or getting unduly attracted to others' skin doesn't make much sense for a wise person. Studying spiritual texts, including the Bhagavad-Gita itself, provides insights into the transient nature of material pleasures and the enduring joy found in spiritual pursuits.
3. *Spiritual Control:* By devotional practices like worship, *mantra* meditation and prayer, one can

develop a higher spiritual consciousness and rise above the desires for lower pleasures. Engaging in spiritual activities not only saves us from addictions and depressing habits but also nourishes us by fostering a more enduring sense of peace and well-being.

4. *Austerity and Moderation:* Engaging in a lifestyle of austerity and moderation in eating and other habits helps in curbing the excesses of lust. Simple living and a balanced approach to sensual pleasures contribute to a more harmonious and disciplined life.

We can transform lust into love by shifting our focus from:

- Mere physical attraction to emotional connection and affection characterized by caring, understanding and empathy
- Immediate gratification of desires to long-term commitment to the well-being and happiness of the beloved
- Self-centred pleasure to sacrifice, selflessness and putting the needs of the loved one before one's own
- Physical intimacy to emotional, intellectual and spiritual intimacy

In essence, the Bhagavad-Gita teaches that controlling lust requires a holistic approach, encompassing spiritual practices, self-discipline and a shift in perspective.

Practices for Inner Balance

1. *Cultivate Mindful Desires:* Stay away from selfish feelings like lust and embrace something selfless like love. Strive to channel desires in a positive spiritual direction.
2. *Choose Favourable Association:* Surround yourself with spiritually minded individuals who promote love and selfless actions, steering clear of associations that induce lusty thoughts.
3. *Prioritize Spiritual Purpose:* Understand that ultimate happiness lies in serving God and fostering spiritual relationships, contributing to the well-being of society, beyond bodily pleasures.
4. *Understand the Dangers of Lust:* Realize that unchecked lust, our inner enemy, can lead to disrupted values, loss of discrimination and moral degradation, causing harm to oneself and others.
5. *Employ Sense Control:* Curb lust by practising sense control through safe distance from lust-inducing visuals, intellectual control through scriptural knowledge and spiritual control through prayer.

11

Rage in the Modern Age

Navigating Justifiable Anger

Once, our cook at the Ecovillage prepared a south Indian dish called uttappa, topping it with small pieces of carrots, beans, chillies, along with some coriander leaves.

When the uttappa was served, I carefully removed all the chilli pieces, since I knew they were beyond my capacity to handle. After enjoying my first bite of the dish with chutney, I took another bite, and suddenly felt a burning sensation on my tongue and in my throat. I was almost in tears and had hiccups. Someone came to my rescue with a cup of water, helping to relieve me. Soon, I realized the cause of this catastrophe—an innocent, small, green bean-like piece that turned out to be a hot chilli!

Chilli is a common ingredient in many meals; some enjoy it, while others find it challenging to take on. When used in a reasonable quantity, it enhances the taste, but

excessive amounts can overpower the dish. Something similar is the case with anger.

> *Just as excessive chilli creates a burning sensation in the throat, intense anger can create a burning sensation in the heart.*
>
> *Just as an appropriate quantity of chilli can add taste to a preparation, an appropriate amount of anger can bring a positive change in a situation.*

Let's explore the dynamics of anger (*krodha*) in detail, but before that, I urge you to consider the following statements of Lord Krishna in the Gita (2.62-63) about the reason and result of anger:

1. Unfulfilled desires lead to anger (*kāmāt krodho 'bhijāyate*)
2. Unbridled anger leads to delusion (*krodhād bhavati sammohah*)

Identifying Good Anger

Can anger ever be good? Well, maybe it can . . .

Anger is a natural emotion that arises in a person when one's desires or expectations are unfulfilled. Such anger is not always bad. If the desires are reasonable, then the anger caused due to unfulfilment of those desires is also reasonable. But when the desires are unreasonable and inappropriate, the resultant anger is unjustified.

For instance, being deprived of a basic facility or entitlement may put us off and that is totally natural. Also,

being snubbed and mistreated unreasonably may cause us to become furious. These responses, although angry in nature, are fully justified.

Suppressed anger could turn into long-term negativity and grudges.

Anger serves as a natural response to injustice or mistreatment. Take the tale of Prince Dhruva who, at the tender age of five, was denied his rightful place on his father's lap by his selfish stepmother. This made Dhruva angry.

Another instance where your anger can be justified is when it becomes a catalyst for positive change. Sometimes, anger has its utility in rectifying a tricky situation or disciplining a mischievous person. While dealing with juniors, we may have to take a stern approach to clarify our point. Also, some interactions may require that we raise our voice for the benefit of another, just as in the case of a teacher correcting a student's mistakes.

Parents may also sometimes get angry with their naughty children, not due to a lack of love, but simply to reform their mischievous acts. But that anger must be proportional to the mistake committed. It must be appropriately channelled and used sparingly. Controlled anger, aimed at correction and discipline, is constructive. Uncontrolled anger, often displayed through shouting and yelling, is destructive and often distances people from us.

Exhibit controlled anger if needed, but don't come under the control of anger.

Just as a spicy chilli has its place in certain preparations, anger has its role in certain situations of life. But it has to be proportionate to the purpose and the person we are dealing with. Different people require varying levels of chilli; similarly, different people and different situations need different levels of anger. To correct a sober person who accidentally makes a mistake, mild feedback would be sufficient. But to correct a rebellious person who deliberately makes mistakes repeatedly, severe feedback or disciplinary action or even corporal punishment may be required.

> *Expressing anger with self-control is beneficial, especially when offering constructive feedback or correcting misbehaviour.*

For example, mighty Hanuman was enraged at Ravana's grave offence of kidnapping Mother Sita. Hanuman burnt all of Lanka, the golden city of Ravana, to teach Ravana a lesson for the crimes he had committed. Another example is the mighty bowman, Arjuna. He directed his anger towards the wicked supporters of Duryodhana in the battle of Kurukshetra. Thus, anger can be used as a productive tool to deal with the arrogant.

> *Channelize your anger for a noble cause, not for a petty ego clash.*

Anger becomes a beneficial force when used judiciously—avoiding overuse or misuse. We need to ensure that we don't come under the sway of anger and lose our

composure. Not every situation demands anger for correction or discipline; hence, it should be employed sparingly and with thoughtful consideration.

While facing insults or addressing misconduct, anger becomes a potent tool, when tempered with discretion and intelligence.

When we refrain from venting our anger for a right purpose, it can possibly lead to inner turmoil. However, mastering the ability to control our anger, especially in the face of trivial ego clashes, will pull us out of the well of negativity and bring us to a place of peace.

The Pitfalls of Unchecked Anger

In the archives of universal history, the tale of King Daksha serves as a stark reminder of how seemingly trivial causes of anger can lead to severe consequences. Once, when Daksha entered a grand assembly filled with several devas and sages, everyone stood up to welcome him. But Lord Shiva didn't stand up to honour him, as he was deeply immersed in meditation. Daksha became furious with Lord Shiva, an exalted personality, superior to Daksha in many ways. Daksha's unwarranted anger, born out of his ego and hunger for honour, made him bitterly criticize and curse Shiva, and even led him to walk out of the grand assembly despite pleas to stay, which was not proper etiquette. Even later, Daksha maintained a similar attitude towards the exalted Shiva. Eventually, he had to pay the heavy price of his head for all his offences to Lord Shiva.

The cause of the anger may be silly, but the consequences can be severe.

Unreasonable anger, often stemming from insignificant triggers, tends to result in destructive outcomes. Thoughtless and arrogant words, such as those wielded by Daksha, can cause irreparable damage. In the heat of anger, exaggeration becomes a common folly, where mistakes are magnified beyond necessity, and false or exaggerated statements are uttered without restraint.

The fundamental principle guiding anger should be its potential to inspire positive change. When anger fails to contribute to improved performance or a positive shift in the situation, it becomes a self-inflicted detriment. Reflecting on this, the basic thumb rule emerges:

The expression of anger should aim for positive transformation rather than regrettable consequences.

Anger is like a wild river that, if left unchecked, can drown the beauty of everything around it.

Imagine your anger as a red balloon held tight in your hand for a long time. Feel the tension slowly easing as you release it, watching it float away into the vast sky. Letting go brings a sense of lightness and freedom, allowing peace to fill the space it once occupied.

When we expect things to happen right or our way, and they don't, we often get angry. Or when we expect someone to behave in a certain way, and they don't, we get absolutely annoyed. So, the best way to enjoy life is to live

it the way it is going. Without intensely desiring to have something our way.

Imagine a theatrical life where every reaction from everyone we meet is scripted. Wouldn't that be a dull life? I assume it would. So, instead of trying to stage our life, we could try housing reasonable expectations and wishes and thereby keep unneeded irritation at bay.

> *Unfulfilled desires and expectations are the two causes of anger.*
>
> *Sometimes, tiny frustrations turn into storms of anger, causing a great deal of stress, and a negative ambience around.*

Now a question may arise: 'What if others get angry with me? How do I deal with that?'

Let's crack the code together.

Dealing with Others' Anger

When people get angry with us, it's crucial to recognize that the words spoken in the heat of the moment may not accurately reflect their true sentiments.

Also, putting on our detective glasses and reading through the anger can help us identify the cause of the outburst. Scanning through the cause can give us a better picture of whether such anger is to be tolerated or not.

> *An angry person often says more than what he or she means. Don't take their words seriously or personally, but empathize with them.*

Oftentimes, by simply being patient and tolerant, we allow the infuriated to purge out and calm down. Acting impulsively in the face of their anger may aggravate the argument and damage the relationship beyond restoration. This could be one of the traumatizing after-effects of dealing with anger angrily!

Once the storm of anger subsides, the one enraged generally feels remorseful, expresses regret and apologizes for their behaviour. *We need to facilitate this transformation with our diligence, patience and forgiveness.* In the intensity of emotion, their words may have surpassed their true intentions, but they may not be inherently bad. However, if the person remains unapologetic and continues to justify their inappropriate behaviour, a measured response in line with the situation would be necessary.

Mistakes are common!
Regret and don't repeat.
Rectify and don't justify.

We need to discern between the person's momentary anger and a persistent refusal to accept one's mistakes, and respond appropriately.

A Balanced Perspective

While the absence of excessive anger is commendable, a total deficiency of anger may indicate indifference or apathy towards injustice. Anger, stemming from genuine emotions, is not inherently negative; rather, it can be a

catalyst for positive change when appropriately channelled in response to perceived injustices.

An illustrative example is found in the tale of King Vena. Although it was his responsibility to take care of his citizens, he tormented them, disrespected the sages and stopped all sacrifices, worship and spiritual activities in his kingdom. His cruelty and self-proclaimed divinity angered both his citizens and the sages advising him. The sages told Vena to stop his atrocities, but Vena arrogantly declined their advice and claimed himself to be God. The sages then directed their justified anger to chant *mantras* to kill Vena, a tyrannical king unfit for his position.

Just as fire burns things on the ground, but not the ground itself, appropriate anger serves as a tool for rectifying negativity without causing harm. It's akin to a parent or a teacher disciplining a child—a necessary expression of care. However, when anger crosses its limits, and the parents or teachers excessively punish the child or are overly harsh with them, that can impede the healthy growth of the child.

Recognizing and appropriately expressing anger is integral to addressing injustices and fostering positive change, ensuring that it serves as a force for correction rather than harm.

A Few Quick Tools to Control Anger

1. *Regulate Desires and Expectations:* Imagine your mind is like a calm and peaceful ocean, and your

wishes are like rivers flowing into it. It's totally fine to have wishes. But if we only think about getting more and more things all the time, it's like too many rivers rushing into our calm ocean. Sometimes, these wishes can't all come true and when that happens, we might feel frustrated and angry. Enjoy the things you already have! You can still have wishes, just not too many all the time.

2. *Mantras to Calm Your Mind:* Chant your favourite *mantra* like '*Om namo bhagavata vasudevaya*' or '*Jai Sri Ram*' or '*Om namo narayanaya*', to help yourself control your anger. Thus, you not only calm down but also access the blessings of the Lord to deal with the situation at hand more effectively.
3. *Talk About It:* Share why you're upset with someone you trust—a friend, a family member or a mentor. Expressing your emotions can be therapeutic and help dissipate anger.
4. *Recognize the Destructive Power of Anger:* Anger stands as a significant threat in both spiritual life and everyday relationships. Throughout history, numerous instances illustrate how individuals have jeopardized their connections and spiritual progress due to momentary lapses in temper. Whenever anger surfaces within us, we should reflect on the potential consequences of giving in to it. By contemplating the potential consequences of giving in to anger, we can find inspiration to maintain a calm and composed demeanour.

The Triad of Destruction

Unfulfilled desires (*kama*) cause anger (*krodha*), and fulfilled desires cause greed (*lobha*). Therefore, Lord Krishna says in the Gita (16.21) that these three qualities are doorways to hell:

tri-vidham narakasyedam
dvāram nāśanam ātmanah
kāmah krodhas tathā lobhas
tasmād etat trayam tyajet

'Desire, anger and greed that lead to degradation are considered three gates leading to this hell. So, they must be given up.'

In essence, by relinquishing these destructive qualities, we can pave our own way for a brighter future.

Practices for Inner Balance

1. *Evaluate Anger's Justifiability:* Reflect on the nature of your desires and expectations to determine if they are reasonable. Anger arising from justified grievances, such as denial of basic facilities or mistreatment, can be reasonable.
2. *Practise Controlled Anger for Positive Change:* Use anger judiciously, as a catalyst for constructive purposes, such as rectifying mistakes or inculcating discipline. Exercise self-control in expressing anger, tailoring its intensity to the purpose and the individual involved.
3. *Foster Positive Transformation through Anger:* Prioritize positive transformation as the goal of expressing anger, rather than causing regrettable consequences. Ensure that anger contributes to improved performance or a positive shift in the situation.
4. *Deal Constructively with Others' Anger:* Understand that words spoken in the heat of the moment may not accurately reflect others' true sentiments. Practise patience and tolerance when dealing with others' anger, facilitating their calm-down and expression of remorse.
5. *Quick Tools to Control Anger:* Maintain a balance between having wishes and appreciating the things you have. Chant *mantras* to calm your mind. Share your feelings with trusted ones. Understand the destructive power of anger.

12

Bridging Hearts with Words

Bitter Words Are Weightless but Often Weigh Down

Have you ever seen an earthen pot? Do you know one of its key features? An earthen pot, once broken, is not reusable. Even if you manage to put the broken pieces of the pot together and make it usable again, you have to be extremely careful in handling that pot, much more than a new pot. Any slight mishandling of such a repaired pot breaks it again and makes it permanently irreparable. Relationships are also somewhat like a pot. Insensitive dealings can sometimes cause irreversible heartbreak.

What comes to your mind when you think of sustainable relationships? Well, life taught me that effective communication plays the role of the binding material holding relationships together for longer. Words play a pivotal role in our interactions. The way we speak can either make or break connections. Being mindful of our

speech fosters positive friendships, while harsh speech seriously disrupts relationships.

In the Bhagavad-Gita (17.6), Lord Krishna, emphasizing the culture of communication, said, '*anudvega-karam vakyam, satyam priya-hitam cayat.*' This statement has three parts.

Our words (*vakyam*) must be:

1. *Anudvega-karam:* Free from causing distress or agitation to others
2. *Satyam:* Truthful
3. *Priya-hitam:* Pleasant and beneficial

When we can mould our speech in accordance to this recommendation of Lord Krishna, we can enjoy fulfilling relationships.

Positive Words Encourage and Empower

Positive words empower and attract others, building strong bonds between people's hearts. The great epic Ramayana illustrates the power of positive words. When the demon king Ravana kidnapped Mother Sita in the absence of Lord Rama, the monkey warriors set out to search for her. While on their search, mighty Hanuman, Jambavan, Angada and many others in their team came to the shore of the ocean in the south. They learnt that Mother Sita was being held captive in Ravana's kingdom Lanka, which lay on the other shore of the ocean. Now their mission was to cross the ocean to reach Lanka.

A wave of disappointment overwhelmed them as they saw the expanse of the ocean. No one felt confident

enough to jump across the one-hundred-*yojanas*-wide ocean (one *yojana* is eight miles). They all were dejected. Some monkeys said that they could jump ten *yojanas*, or twenty, thirty, forty, and so on. One of them named Angada claimed to be able to jump one hundred *yojanas*, but he doubted he could do it a second time to return.

It was then that the wise and elderly Jambavan spoke. 'Do not worry. We have Hanuman, who is fully capable of performing this most difficult feat. O Hanuman, you are equal to Garuda, the carrier of Lord Vishnu. Why have you not spoken up? You are the best of all monkeys. You are the son of the mighty wind god, Vayu. You have received special boons from Lord Brahma and Indra, and thus became invincible. Now is the time for you to exhibit your power.'

Thus, Jambavan praised Hanuman in various ways, reminding him of his extraordinary strength. This motivated Hanuman who then expanded himself into a gigantic form and prepared for a massive leap across the ocean. A genuine well-wisher is the one who identifies the strengths in others, and inspires and encourages them.

> *Genuine appreciation empowers, encourages and strengthens a person, while fault-finding disempowers, discourages and weakens one's determination. Unnecessary fault-finding makes the faults true even if they didn't exist before.*

A contrasting example is found in the story of the celebrated Prince Dhruva. Once when five-year-old Dhruva attempted to sit on his father's lap, his stepmother

Suruchi prevented him from doing so. 'You are not qualified to sit there, because you are not born of my womb,' she said. 'You are the son of an unfortunate woman. If you still wish to sit on your father's throne, you worship Lord Vishnu, and by his blessings, you may take birth in my womb in your next life!' Suruchi's rude and insensitive words pierced Dhruva's heart and agitated his tender mind. He became vengeful towards Suruchi, and developed an ambition to attain a position that no one in the entire universe had ever attained!

> *While pleasing words bring out the best in others, harsh words bring out the worst in them.*

Caloric Speech: I believe words of flattery to be something like extra calories. Initially, they may taste sweet but eventually, they end up thickening the waistline. This is because a flatterer often has an agenda to fulfil and bears selfish interests. A selfless person genuinely appreciates others, desires their well-being and rejoices in their successful endeavours. The words of such people help us reach our full potential.

But sometimes we wonder whether our words should be truthful or beneficial. Well, here's the fix.

Speaking Truthfully vs Speaking Beneficially

Before leaping across the Lanka Ocean, to encourage the despondent monkeys, Hanuman said, 'I can circle Mount Meru a thousand times without pausing. By splashing

the ocean waters, I can inundate the entire world. I can circumambulate Garuda a thousand times as he flies in the sky. I can uproot the entire city of Lanka.' All the monkeys were thrilled.

> *Sometimes, to give much-needed reassurance to a dejected person, a wise person boasts about his powers, but without false pride. That induces hope and confidence in the discouraged hearts.*

The same Hanuman, upon meeting Sitadevi in Lanka, encouraged her differently. Sita wondered if the other monkey soldiers could cross the ocean and reach Lanka like Hanuman. To reassure her, Hanuman said, 'All the monkeys in our army are equal or superior to me! Surely, they will all easily reach Lanka. It is only inferior persons like me who are sent as messengers.'

Hanuman is certainly not an inferior soldier, and hardly anyone was equal to him or better than him in his army. His words were certainly not truthful, but practical. Hanuman, who, to give hope to the monkeys, had boasted of his prowess before crossing the ocean, downplayed his prowess after crossing the ocean, to give hope to Sitadevi. These two cases might seem contradictory, but in both cases, Hanuman's purpose was to encourage and reassure the despondent. This is how a mature person induces hope in others with well-wishing and sensible words.

> *Focus not just on truthful words, but practical, beneficial, sensitive and well-wishing words.*

There are times, though, when we have to present a refusal or say no; wouldn't doing that be mean and hurtful?

Sensitive Speech in Delicate Situations

In life, we often encounter situations requiring delicate communication. For instance, we may have to convey to someone the loss of a close friend or a significant setback in business or extend a sincere apology for a non-undoable mistake. Or sometimes, we may have to reject an offer or say no to a sincere request, due to various constraints.

In such situations, it's important to carefully choose the words and tone, something like choosing our car and its colour. While it may be challenging, it is vital to express these truths with great care, ensuring we don't disturb the peace of mind of those we're communicating with.

The tone of our words plays a pivotal role, often surpassing the importance of the content itself.

Even positive news, when conveyed in an unpleasant and neglectful manner, leaves a negative impact. On the other hand, negative news, if communicated with sensitivity, can make people more open to accepting even the most difficult truths. Whether we have to share unpleasant news with someone or say no to their sincere request or express our disinclination to fulfil their needs, we need to communicate with sensitivity and sincerity.

We may not always give a positive response, but we must give a sensitive response.

Therefore, the choice of our words and the tone we adopt are paramount in our interactions. And this is possible only when we cultivate a well-wishing heart. When we genuinely desire the well-being of others, we naturally become attuned to their situations. This sensitivity allows us to speak the right words, appropriate to the occasion. Let's earnestly strive to be genuine well-wishers, fostering understanding in our communication with those around us.

Choice of Words—A Strategy or A Mindset?

Lord Krishna advocated for speech that doesn't agitate (*anudvega-karam vakyam*) in the above verse. Yet, before even beginning His philosophical teachings of the Bhagavad-Gita, Lord Krishna sternly rebuked Arjuna for his despondency about fighting in the Kurukshetra battle, seemingly contradicting His teaching. However, this apparent inconsistency is justified.

A well-wishing heart precedes speaking pleasant words.

There are instances where elders, teachers or parents may need to express themselves strongly to instigate positive transformation in the hearts of their dependants. Parents might need to correct their children, teachers may have to provide strong feedback to students or senior figures in an organization may need to address serious mistakes by juniors. In such cases, using assertive language becomes necessary, given the circumstances.

While polite and gentle speech is generally preferred, there are situations where a softer approach might not be feasible. Parents and teachers, by default, are considered genuine well-wishers of their dependants and are thus authorized to speak assertively when required. However, not everyone has the authority or necessity to use strong language with others. In most circumstances, cultivating a truthful and considerate communication style is advisable, combining sincerity with a gentle manner. So, using the right words is not a mere strategy but an expression of a well-wishing heart.

The Power of Silence

Effective communication extends beyond speaking with a positive mindset; it involves recognizing the power of silence. It's not mandatory to respond to every comment or question.

Have you ever wondered why people shout during heated-up arguments, although they are close to each other? The tendency to raise their voices often stems from the emotional distance created despite physical proximity. This phenomenon occurs because, in order to convey a point, individuals feel compelled to exert extra energy and volume to ensure their message reaches the other person's ears, mind and heart. Conversely, those who share love and cooperation can communicate softly even when physically apart, as their emotional closeness transcends the need for loud speech.

It is crucial to discern when not to speak, especially during intense disagreements, when opinions escalate into verbal quarrels. In such situations, embracing silence can defuse tension, prompting the other party to follow suit. If both individuals persist in bitter exchanges, the quarrel intensifies, straining relationships. Therefore, understanding the art of strategic silence is essential for fostering understanding and maintaining healthy connections.

Sometimes, although we don't indulge in arguments, we may tend to speak on unnecessary topics. Inappropriate use of speech, especially on mundane or negative topics, adds little value and may fill the atmosphere with unproductive vibrations. Time is a limited resource, urging individuals to speak constructively and avoid engaging in discussions that contribute to negativity and waste precious energy. We can invest our time wisely by engaging in meaningful conversations, studying wisdom texts and learning from wise people, thereby nurturing personal growth and contributing positively to the world.

Would you like to build bridges with your words, or walls? The choice is yours!

Practices for Inner Balance

1. *Practise Mindful Communication:* Be conscious of your words and their potential impact on others. Prioritize speech that is free from causing distress, truthful, pleasant and beneficial.
2. *Cultivate Positive Words:* Encourage and empower others through genuine appreciation, identify their strengths and inspire them with well-wishing and sensible words.
3. *Speak Sensitively:* Approach delicate communications with care, especially when delivering unpleasant news or refusing requests. Choose words and tone wisely to express truths without disturbing others' peace.
4. *Embrace Strategic Silence:* Understand the power of silence in defusing tension during disagreements. Recognize when not to speak, avoiding unnecessary topics that contribute to negativity.

13

Beyond the Masks

Rediscovering Truth in a Hypocritical World

When I was studying in the fourth grade, on one holiday, I played with my friends the whole day. As a result, I was quite dirty by the end of the day. In the evening, while I was on the street with a few other kids, my mother called me home. She had noticed my dishevelled appearance. I understood why she was calling me and went to her.

She remarked, 'You look so dirty! Go and take a bath immediately.'

Admitting to my untidy state, I replied, 'Yes, I am shabby. But I will take a bath later. I am in the midst of an interesting game.'

'You have been playing for the whole day anyway,' she said, and pointed out to some of my friends who looked fresh. 'Do you see, they've taken a bath and have put on clean clothes. Are you not ashamed?'

Before she could speak another word, I realized the contrast between their freshness and my dirty appearance and suggested, 'Give me some face powder; I'll apply it to look fresh in front of my friends. Currently, I don't have the time for a bath; I need to get back to playing.'

This annoyed my mother and she responded, 'Are you not ashamed of saying this? If you apply powder, you may look fresh from a distance, but when people come close to you, they will realize how stinky you are. Don't try to deceive people by appearing clean; actually become clean. Go and take a bath immediately.'

I got my dose and lesson, and immediately headed to the bathroom.

The World of Deception

When my mother instructed me to take a bath, her emphasis was on not just *appearing* fresh but *actually* being fresh. This idea can extend beyond physical cleanliness to inner purity as well. When the mind or heart is clean with pure intentions, noble thoughts and virtuous desires, we can lead a more peaceful life even amidst chaos. Such consciousness facilitates fulfilling relationships.

Imagine conversing with a person to fulfil a selfish purpose while trying to impress him with multiple exaggerated promises and flattery. Compare and contrast it with having an open-hearted conversation with a friend with no agenda but just sharing your honest and heartfelt feelings. In which case would you feel more stressed

and anxious? In which case would you feel happier and more peaceful?

We are often influenced by the false propaganda, bombardments, trends and temptations of this world that allure us to pursue unworthy things. They don't give us enduring happiness but keep us in an illusory state or utopian world of imaginary pleasures. And by speaking flowery words, we also consciously or unconsciously keep others in illusion.

Oftentimes, those who try to fool others are themselves fooled by the forces of the world.

Strategized Relationships

Consider a situation where you've committed a mistake and are trying to hide from your family or society, and even succeed in doing so. Now compare it with the case where you honestly admit your mistake, apologize for it, rectify it and resolve not to repeat it. Which is more relieving and comforting?

In the Bhagavad-Gita, Lord Krishna repeatedly stresses having a clean heart, devoid of duplicity, hypocrisy and deceitful tendencies, and explains their dangers. He urges us to cultivate honesty and integrity in our interactions and thus enliven our relationships.

Cultivating healthy relationships is NOT a strategy.

It requires a heartfelt desire more than strategy, tips and techniques. Of course, there are some basic practices like

polite speech, frequency of meetings, greeting on special occasions, supporting others when they need us, wishing people on their birthdays, encouraging them during setbacks and so on, but if all these aspects of interaction are used only as strategies without genuine love, affection and concern in the heart, such relationships are not sustainable. While many people often look for strategies to improve interactions, the fundamental ingredient for meaningful connections is love.

> *Genuine love and appreciation for people and valuing them for what they are naturally foster strong and lasting relationships.*

For instance, to give feedback to someone, a common strategy of 'plus-minus-plus' is followed by many. This involves a thoughtful approach that starts off by appreciating the good work done, then providing the necessary corrections for the mistakes that happened, and concluding positively with some encouraging words. This method aims to make feedback more appealing, digestible, relatable and acceptable, without making the person feel offended. However, beyond the 'plus-minus-plus' strategy, the effectiveness of feedback lies in genuine concern, love and a sincere desire for the improvement of the recipient. A genuine wish for others' betterment, when combined with the plus-minus-plus strategy, can be more transformative and meaningful, fostering deeper relationships.

In the absence of a genuine intention for others' improvement, merely sticking to a feedback strategy may require careful consideration of word choice. On the other hand, when there is trust, genuine intentions and a positive attitude, even if the plus-minus-plus strategy is not strictly followed, suggestions and feedback are likely to be respected, valued and accepted.

My mother scolded me several times when I erred, but she hardly followed a plus-minus-plus strategy. Despite the strong feedback, my faith in her remained intact; I fully trusted her intentions and believed that she was my well-wisher beyond doubt. Lord Krishna began His teachings of the Gita by first heavily criticizing Arjuna's weakness of heart in not being inclined to fight. Arjuna wasn't offended by Lord Krishna's criticism, but accepted Him as his guru, and requested Him for guidance to clear his confusion. Arjuna had full faith in Lord Krishna as a genuine well-wisher.

Of course, an average individual cannot be a well-wisher of others as much as the Supreme Father, Lord Krishna, or a loving mother, but at least we can strive to value and respect people genuinely, and at least not succumb to deceiving, disrespecting or cheating them for our selfish interests, in the garb of being well-wishers.

Genuine intentions and a positive attitude can make feedback more effective and accepted, transcending the need for rigid strategies.

Emotions behind Expressions

Upon receiving a favour, we may say, 'Thank you!' But without genuinely *feeling grateful* for the good that a person has done to us, simply *mumbling a thanks* externally doesn't strengthen our relationship. Relationships are not just based on expressions, but *heartfelt* expressions! Without emotional bonding, formal expressions have little value and effect.

> *Expressing gratitude goes beyond words; it must align with genuine feelings to endure.*

Similarly, presenting ourselves in an externally appealing manner without developing the necessary internal qualities lacks substance. Instead of focusing solely on impressing others externally, we can try working on our internal state—our mood, attitude and consciousness.

The world may tempt you to employ strategies to cultivate relationships by using flattery and gifts even without genuine goodwill. But relationships flourish by fostering a sincere and genuine concern for others, and a well-wishing heart devoid of duplicity.

How long can we impress people with our techniques, diplomacy, strategies and external appeal? Sooner or later, our inner consciousness will reveal itself. So, let's focus on cultivating the right inner mood by acknowledging their significance in our lives and relationships.

Pursuing Genuineness

Imagine an orchestra with multiple musicians playing different instruments as the lead singer sings a captivating

song. What if the instruments don't sound in harmony with the singer? Can the audience have a pleasant experience? I don't think so. It's the harmony amongst them that makes the musical performance appealing, memorable and fulfilling to both the performers and the audience.

Similarly, when there is no harmony between our emotions, expressions and actions, there can't be any fulfilment or genuine satisfaction in life's journey. So, spiritual culture guides us towards genuineness and honesty. It recommends that we develop integrity and align what we do with what we speak, and what we speak with what we think. Diplomacy, duplicity and hypocrisy spoil the experience of life's journey, while integrity, honesty and genuineness enrich life's journey. These very qualities make us trustworthy and reliable for people and brighten our relationships. But people who constantly try to impress or manipulate others without being genuine struggle to build lasting relationships. True connections are based on honesty and trust, not just flattery or manipulation. Without sincerity, relationships lack depth and are more likely to be short-lived.

> *Integrity is to align our expressions, actions and emotions.*

Throughout the Gita, Lord Krishna urges us to develop the virtues of honesty, humility, integrity, compassion, truthfulness, cleanliness, detachment. We may not develop all these qualities overnight just by doing a single read

of the Bhagavad-Gita. This is because it is an ongoing process where we keep upgrading ourselves gradually with determined effort as our propeller.

Are you ready to take your first baby step?

Work in Progress

Picture a construction site filled with various materials: bricks, cement, tiles, iron and more. This site may be noisy and disruptive, making it challenging to have a peaceful conversation or focus on work. However, it's a work-in-progress site, and the erection of a building is expected. One apartment will be ready for you to comfortably work in, sleep, converse and enjoy yourself. But this will take the combined efforts of the engineers, masons and labour.

Our lives mirror this construction site—a continuous work in progress. Just as a building starts with a foundation and grows into a multistorey structure, our lives begin with basic understanding and experience, and we evolve into more mature individuals with increased understanding, intelligence and wisdom.

While still growing, we may make mistakes and not exhibit the greatest character and wisdom immediately. Yet, persistent efforts with integrity and determination lead to maturity. Similar to a building's completion requiring collaboration from engineers, machines and labour, our maturity is influenced by various people—teachers, friends, family and parents—contributing to our growth.

Smartly benefiting from experienced individuals and reading wisdom texts like the Bhagavad-Gita equip us

with essential life philosophy. Maturity, unlike a product on sale, is cultivated through learning, sincere application of wisdom in practical life and leveraging the support of those around us.

In the Gita, Lord Krishna emphasized that the development of qualities such as compassion, integrity, gratitude, kindness, tolerance and satisfaction is essential. Following a spiritual path can foster these virtues. Ultimately, *bhakti*, or devotion, forms the basis for cultivating these qualities. So, let's work at the root and observe our life turn into a fulfilling and mature one.

Practices for Inner Balance

1. *Cultivate Inner Purity:* Regularly reflect on your intentions, thoughts and desires, and strive to come closer to purity, for a more peaceful and fulfilling life amidst external chaos.
2. *Strive for Sincerity over Strategy:* Cultivate genuine concern, care, compassion and appreciation in relationships over basic practices like polite speech and support, or strategies to impress people.
3. *Emphasize Genuine Intentions in Feedback:* Combine your feedback with honest concern, positive intentions and desire for the improvement of the other person, to foster trust in relationships.
4. *Express Gratitude with Genuine Feelings:* Thank people with true appreciation for their contributions rather than relying solely on formal expressions and impressive words.
5. *Strive for Genuineness and Integrity:* Align your expressions, actions and emotions with honesty and integrity, in both your personal and professional life, to build trust and reliability in relationships.

14

Threads of Unity

Navigating Spiritual Love and Material Prejudice

What if we had the eyes of a camera? Clicking and capturing multiple pictures—pictures of different people, places, foods and much more. With an unbiased vision that appreciates the beauty of difference; a vision that puts the big and small, tall and short, fit and fat—all into one frame. Of course, a camera has no emotions and wisdom. But I was imagining a vision that's non-judgemental and devoid of prejudice but with natural wisdom and fair emotions!

There was an experience that led me to this thought. Let me rewind a little and take you to the day when my beloved Guru, His Holiness Radhanath Swami, was delivering a spiritual discourse at the Ecovillage. A couple of questions had long been buzzing through my head and I was curious to have them answered.

'Does a spiritualist need to cancel out all attachments before setting forth on the path of spirituality?'

'Must those dedicated to God love only Him and no one else?'

But before I could raise these questions, the beautiful words of my beloved Guru answered them in just one profound sentence:

> *'One who truly loves God loves everyone who loves God, loves everyone who tries to love God, and loves everyone whom God loves.'*

This statement almost put me on pause. It compelled me to think. It also unfolded four dimensions of spiritual life that are ultimately meant to awaken love for God in the heart of a spiritualist.

The four dimensions are:

1. Loving the Lord Himself with great dedication and devotion
2. Loving the unflinching devotees of the Lord who exclusively surrender unto Him
3. Loving those who are practising the spiritual path, striving to invoke their inherent love for God—these are not yet perfect devotees but are on the path to perfection
4. Loving those whom God loves; that means loving every living entity in this world. Because everyone is a child of God

> *God hates no one, how then can a lover of God hate anyone?*

Who Is a Real Spiritualist?

Since God loves every living entity as His child, truly God-loving persons also extend their love to everyone and everything connected to God. Is there anything in this entire creation of God that is not connected to Him? Absolutely nothing! So, the real spiritualists are those who hold no prejudice or discrimination towards anyone or anything. They hate no one but treat everyone with love and kindness without any other consideration.

This understanding of spirituality left me mesmerized, and I couldn't help but admire the profound wisdom encapsulated in my Guru's statement. I naturally reflected on it deeper and longer!

> *Spiritual vision promotes love and kindness, while material vision supports prejudice and discrimination.*

In the course of time, some humble contemplation on my Guru's statement led me to recollect one profound verse from the Bhagavad-Gita (5.18) where Lord Krishna says:

vidyā-vinaya-sampanne
brāhmaṇe gavi hastini
śuni caiva śva-pāke ca
paṇḍitāḥ sama-darśinaḥ

'Those who are endowed with mature knowledge and yet are humble at heart, see a brāhmaṇa, a cow, an elephant, a dog and a dog-eater with an equal vision.'

This *shloka* encourages conflict resolution and promotes the unification of humanity beyond all external

differences of nationality, ethnicity, race and religion. While we need to acknowledge natural differences among people, what's more important is to recognize their connection with God. This is a simple way to rise above a discriminative vision.

'But how am I connected to a weird-looking animal or a stranger?'

'Without an apparent connection, how am I supposed to love such entities?'

If these are your questions, here's the answer.

The Spirit-Matter Link

There is a natural link between humans, animals and so on. They are all spiritual beings enveloped in a material body. Furthermore, on a spiritual plane, they are cherished children of God, the Supreme Almighty, who loves them all equally. Lord Krishna says in the Bhagavad-Gita, 'Material nature is the mother of all living beings, and I am the seed-giving father' (14.4).

Thus, He looks at all living beings, His children, with an equal vision. Therefore, for a spiritualist, this spiritual equality becomes the focal point, emanating from the understanding that everyone is a spirit soul and a fragmental part of God. Ultimately, seeing everyone as children of God fosters compassion.

Just as God refrains from discrimination, a lover of God adopts an equal vision, seeing the divine connection in all.

A wise person acknowledges the spiritual equality among all beings, behind their material differences. Even examining it from a material perspective, there exists an equality among different living beings. The bodies of all living beings, whether sheep, dog or human, are composed of the same fundamental material elements—earth, water, fire, air and ether.

'But what is the advantage of taking to this spiritual vision? How can it change my life?'

The Empathetic Me

Slowly, as we begin to observe the divine connection we have with every living entity around us, our vision begins to deepen. We notice everyone dealing with hunger, pleasure, pain, love and various other emotions that show up in almost everyone. In time, this vision translates into universal empathy and compassion. Flushing down our grudges and negativity becomes so much easier. And in the end, we find ourselves transformed into more appreciative and compassionate people. Most importantly, when we develop a compassionate and well-wishing attitude towards everyone, it fills our own hearts with a feeling of joy and satisfaction.

> *Spiritual life never promotes indifference and violence towards others, rather it promotes love and compassion for all, on the basis of love for the Supreme.*

Soon, our inclinations change. We start feeling for others. Technically, this state is called *para dukha dukhi*—or a

state of considering others unhappiness as one's own. Eventually, people around us are inspired and benefited by such behaviour, and in turn, all of us together lay the foundation of an organic society—where every living entity is loved and cared for.

Empathy makes us extraordinary well-wishers of society.

Chaos Caused by Bias and Prejudice

In our world, chaos often stems from a failure to recognize the spiritual equality among all living beings. Despite the fundamental similarity in the basic ingredients of our physical bodies and the inherent spiritual connection each individual shares with the Divine, discriminatory practices based on factors such as caste, creed, gender, nationality and social status persist. Beyond the material realm, every individual is inherently a spiritual being, intrinsically connected to the Almighty Lord, fostering a shared sense of interconnectedness among all living beings.

Despite this inherent unity, the world grapples with pervasive discrimination, division and inequality. Caste-based biases, religious prejudices, gender disparities, nationalistic divides and socio-economic distinctions continue to plague societies, contributing to an environment of discord and unrest.

Recognizing and understanding the spiritual vision of equality is crucial for fostering harmony and peace.

Spiritual vision entails acknowledging that beneath the diverse exteriors of human existence, there exists a

common thread of shared humanity and spiritual essence. This recognition should prompt a shift in perspective, transcending superficial differences and embracing the inherent equality that arises from our common origin and spiritual interconnectedness.

Equal vision transcends the limitations of narrow-minded beliefs and prejudices. It calls for cultivating a mindset that appreciates diversity as a manifestation of the divine plan, recognizing that each individual contributes to the rich tapestry of human experience.

But you may have a reasonable question: 'How can I forcefully ignore apparent differences between people? Wouldn't it be foolish to adopt an equal vision?'

Is Discrimination a Sin?

Once, on a festive occasion, we enjoyed a lavish feast featuring a variety of delicious dishes, including my beloved milk sweets. Filled with excitement, I indulged in an excess of these treats, forgetting that the body has its limits when it comes to processing and digesting food. Just as undereating can leave us weak, overeating has its consequences. The aftermath of my enthusiastic consumption became apparent, and I found myself feeling uncomfortably heavy. The realization struck, prompting me to skip dinner that night.

The consequences of my overindulgence became even more apparent the next day when I experienced a bout of diarrhea. A visit to the doctor confirmed that the culprit was undoubtedly the excessive consumption of milk sweets. The prescribed remedy was a small tablet along

with a simple diet consisting of curd rice and buttermilk for the day.

Reflecting on the situation, I couldn't help but marvel at the irony—the same milk that had made me unwell in the form of sweets was now being recommended in the form of curd to aid my recovery. This reminded me of another incident when someone developed a sore throat from consuming chilled ice cream and cold lassi. In that case, the doctor had advised hot milk with ginger and pepper as the remedy.

It's intriguing how the fundamental ingredient, milk, can have contrasting effects depending on its preparation and context. In one instance, it led to indulgence and sickness, while in another, it served as a remedy to restore balance.

> *Equal vision fosters empathy, but blind vision causes disharmony in life. We cannot afford to ignore the self-evident differences among people, things, food items or places!*

Don't Ignore the Self-evident Differences

While the concept of equal vision encourages seeing everyone with equal regard, we can't forcefully ignore the apparent differences between people and treat them in the same way. For instance, a mother cannot reasonably provide her fifth-grade daughter and eighth-grade son with the same set of textbooks, given their distinct academic needs and levels

of comprehension. Likewise, a person responsible for serving food cannot uniformly offer everyone the same quantity of rice and chapatti and assert that it constitutes equal treatment.

> *In navigating life's situations, the essence of equal vision lies not in absolute uniformity but in acknowledging and accommodating relevant differences.*

As humans, we have hierarchical positioning systems categorizing us into juniors and seniors, youngsters and the elderly, children and parents, students and teachers, employees and employers, and so on. Based on this classification, our treatment of people also varies. For instance, a child needs a loving pat on the back, while a high-profile government official or a celebrity requires a more formal and reverential form of appreciation.

> *Appropriate discrimination is essential for maintaining order in society.*

Even amongst the animals there are the carnivorous and the herbivorous. Thus, they are not on the same level. You can go to a *goshala* (cow barn) and hug a cute calf, but you can't go to the forest and embrace a ferocious lion, can you? If someone dares to do so, it would probably be the last hug of their life!

> *Unless we have appropriate discrimination between morality and immorality, our artificial sense of equality only creates disturbance in society.*

When people do good, we need to appreciate them, but when they do bad, we need to disapprove of them, no matter who they are. As a *kshatriya*, Arjuna was socially bound to protect his kingdom from aggressors. But seeing his very own relatives lined up against him had dampened his warrior spirit.

Had Arjuna posed the following question to himself, 'Would I have fought the people I see had they not been my relatives?', he certainly would have said yes. In this way, Arjuna could have prevented his vision from being tainted with personal attachment, eventually leading him to fulfil his *kshatriya* duty.

Similarly, as we acknowledge and act upon external differences in the light of a spiritual connection, we live 'equal vision' to its truest meaning.

> *True equal vision lies in reciprocating with people according to their needs and moods, rather than treating everyone literally equally.*

The world is an ocean of diversity, and that doesn't mean that we simply overlook all the vibrancy that lies before our eyes.

Celebrate the Diversity in Unity

Once, in our temple, I had the opportunity to see some garland makers hold on to a string while moving their hands swiftly and expertly. In no time, an attractively vibrant flower garland was created.

Now, this garland, adorned with petals and flowers of various colours, along with green leaves, looked amazing

on the divine deity of Lord Krishna on the altar. Even single-colour garlands possess a certain beauty, but imagine if everyone offered deities garlands of the same colour and type throughout the year—wouldn't it look monotonous? Therefore, diversity adds to excitement.

And I wondered, 'Just as the unity of flowers of diverse sizes, shapes, colours and fragrances creates a beautiful garland for the Lord's Deity in the temple, wouldn't society become beautiful by accommodating people with diverse backgrounds, talents and skill sets?'

Diversity drives away the monotony and brings flavour to life.

Without diverse food items, a restaurant's menu card wouldn't be exciting to the visitor. Although we may argue that a new addition to the menu could make choosing between dishes more difficult, the very fact that we can choose is because there is a diverse range of dishes to choose from. Similarly, without diversity, smartphone displays would be black and white and so would the world we live in.

When all of us work in harmony while accommodating inevitable differences, we experience greater pleasure in life.

Diversity contributes to beauty if there is harmony.

Unity in Variety

What if all the fingers on your hand were of equal size, length and thickness? Such uniformity would hinder the hand's ability to function properly. Therefore, a hand looks

beautiful and functions well when it possesses fingers of different sizes, shapes and functionalities.

So, it makes sense to celebrate the variety and diversity in the world, while acknowledging unity on the spiritual plane. Real unity is achieved when we acknowledge our spiritual equality as children of God.

> *Only by perceiving and pursuing our eternal relationship with the Supreme Lord Krishna can we attain true equality.*

Consider the example of the Pandavas; the eldest among them, Yudhishthira, was known for his understanding of *Dharma*. He was the personification of moral principles, ethics, values and virtues.

The second brother, Bhima, was renowned for his ability to accomplish herculean tasks and immense physical strength. It is said that each of his arms possessed the strength of 10,000 elephants!

Do you know what this means? Consider 10,000 elephants lined up together. If Bhima punches the first elephant, it would cause the 10,000th elephant to fall. That was his power. Just imagine what must have happened to the first elephant!

The third brother, Arjuna, was a great archer, celebrated for his balance, precision and cleverness. He held a special place as the dearest friend of Lord Krishna, who served as his chariot driver on the battlefield of Kurukshetra. Arjuna's self-control and military prowess earned him certificates of recognition from his guru,

Drona, the king of heaven, Indra, and the greatest of the *devas*, Lord Shiva.

The twins, Nakul and Sahadev, too possessed unique talents and skills. The qualities of the Pandavas were diverse, with each brother known for possessing unique strengths. Despite these differences, they stuck together like the five fingers of a hand. Throughout their lives, they functioned as one single unit, with their mother Kunti as their constant guidepost.

The Pandava brothers were united in purpose, despite having different tastes, talents and working styles. They were united by their love for Lord Krishna.

Spiritually, we are children of the same divine God. While material differences exist, these distinctions are causes for celebration, contributing to the variety within the group rather than causing disparity and conflict.

Unity in diversity should be a cause for celebration, not conflict.

Embracing diversity while acknowledging spiritual unity creates a harmonious and beautiful world.

One who loves God loves everyone who loves God and loves everyone whom God loves.

Practices for Inner Balance

1. *Acknowledge Spiritual Equality:* Recognize that every living being, regardless of background, species, gender, nationality or other external differences, is a child of God.
2. *Promote Empathy and Compassion:* Try to consider others' pain and happiness as your own, and try to cause them happiness and not pain. Strive to be a well-wisher for others, extending help and understanding to alleviate the struggles of fellow beings as much as you can.
3. *Practise Love and Kindness:* Foster an attitude of love and kindness towards everyone, transcending external differences, on the basis of your and their default connection with God.
4. *Balance Equality and Discernment:* Respect individual uniqueness and acknowledge self-evident differences such as qualifications, experiences and hierarchies, knowing well that equal vision doesn't imply literal equal treatment.
5. *Celebrate Diversity in Unity:* Acknowledge the spiritual unity that binds all of us, and recognize that diverse qualities, talents and working styles can coexist harmoniously when directed towards a common purpose and contribute to the overall richness of society.

15

Soulful Soundscapes

Finding Tranquillity through Spiritual Music

During my Bachelor's programme, I found one of my classmates constantly singing a song, particularly the first few lines of the intro. He'd sing it while walking alone, during a casual conversation and even during meals. At home, he would play the cassette and listen to it either through the loudspeakers or headphones. While sitting in class, he would even scribble a few words of the song in his book! For a couple of weeks since the album's release, the song was his constant companion. We used to tease him in a friendly way for his obsession with the song. But we noticed that he seemed really happy and excited while singing it. The underlying current of the song's excitement was evident in everything he did. The song gained popularity due to its captivating music, even though its meaning wasn't so profound.

I, too, found myself getting hooked to certain songs, captivated either by their meaning or by their melody. Consciously or involuntarily, humming a favourite song keeps one excited and joyful, and helps one soothe and calm the mind amidst the chaos of life. I'm pretty sure this is a mutual experience.

Music in general has wonderful therapeutic potential. Music has consistently occupied a revered position, standing as a profoundly influential medium with the power to inspire our hearts. A multitude of studies has cast light on music's remarkable capacity to reduce stress, uplift one's mood and enhance overall emotional well-being. The rhythm, melody and harmonious interplay within music possess the remarkable ability to evoke powerful emotional responses, thereby establishing it as an invaluable tool to find calm in the chaos of this world.

Different songs have different effects on the mind, depending on one's taste and nature. While a song excites some people for a long time, it bores some people or irritates others even on first hearing. Some songs are very melodious but not meaningful, and the lyrics of some songs are inspiring but the music may not be impressive. But some songs captivate both our mind and intellect with their melody and meaning, and remain in our memories for long time.

While the meaning of a song inspires the intellect, its melody attracts the mind. Together, a well-composed, meaningful song enlivens us.

Did you ever wonder if there are any songs that kept people engaged and excited for a long, long time?

History proves that spiritual music and songs composed centuries ago are remembered and adored by people even today for the inspiration and peace they provide. This shows the relevance of spiritual music in dealing with the chaos of life. With adequate personal experience and recurrent observation, I can confidently say that spiritual music helps us in calming the mind amidst the chaos of this world, much more than many other means. Let's explore the finer nuances of spiritual music and delve deep into its distinctive merits.

Facets of Spiritual Music

Oftentimes people use the words *mantra*, *shloka*, *kirtana*, *bhajana*, *prarthana*, *dhyana*, *japa*, meditation, chanting, prayer, recitation, devotional music and so on interchangeably. There is certainly an overlap amongst these processes, and they often aim at the same goal of mental peace and spiritual connection. Yet, there are some finer differences in these processes, knowing which we can get the proper benefit of these precious gifts of the spiritual culture.

Mantra—That which Calms the Mind

Man means 'mind'. *Tra* means to free or liberate. *Man-tra* means 'that which frees the mind'. *Mantra* is a word or a statement which, when continuously repeated or recollected, calms the mind (*mananāt trāyatē iti mantrah*).

Mantra is that which frees the mind by regulating it (*manas trāyatē iti mantrah*).

But aren't freedom and regulation antonyms? The answer is here: A *mantra* frees the mind from all unwanted thoughts, anxieties, agitations, desires or misconceptions, by restricting the mind from overly dwelling on them and by giving the mind a positive subject to dwell upon.

Mantras typically contain the names of the Almighty Lord, the Supreme Divine. Chanting or meditating on prescribed spiritual *mantras* like '*Om namo narayanaya*', '*Om namo bhagavate vasudevaya*' and so on protects us by yielding several beneficial results such as improved concentration, peace and, ultimately, a connection with God.

> One who takes the shelter of a mantra can focus on things that are worthy and meaningful, and divert the mind from unworthy subjects.

Shloka—A Wisdom-Packed Verse

A *shloka* is a verse, a piece of poetry composed in a standard format called *chandas,* which conveys a philosophical truth, a moral teaching, a spiritual principle, a name or a quality of God, or a simple description of a story.

There are multiple types of *chandas*, and accordingly, the verses have a multiple number of syllables, typically arranged in two or four lines. A *shloka* from a holy scripture like the Gita, Ramayana, Mahabharata, Bhagavata Purana and so on conveys philosophical, moral and spiritual teachings, or just narrates the storyline in

poetry. Many *shlokas* simply describe the qualities of the Supreme Lord, who is thus called *Uttama-shloka* or 'one who is glorified in choicest poetry'. Great saints and scholars often study and explain *shlokas* for their deeper meanings and implications.

> Many shlokas are like compressed files that, when unpacked, reveal deep insights and life lessons.

Kirtana—Glorification of God

Kirti means 'glory', 'fame' or 'greatness'. *Kirtana* means to glorify or praise someone's greatness.

A *kirtana* can be in the form of speaking or singing, prose or poetry. Let's say, if I praise Lord Rama's glorious qualities and activities in a discourse, that is called *kirtana*. Or if I sing a song describing His wonderful names and forms, that is also *kirtana*. *Kirtana* can be just chanting the *mantras* that describe the names of the Lord in the form of sweet singing.

When multiple people sing the names and qualities of the Lord together, congregationally, it is called *sankirtana*. *Kirtana* or *sankirtana* can be accompanied by musical instruments and dancing, to enhance the spiritual musical experience of the lead singer, participants and the Lord Himself. Absorption in *kirtanas* gives relief from mental stress and enhances emotional stability by creating a loving bonding with the Lord and invokes the Lord's protection. Therefore, Lord Krishna says in the Gita: '*satatam kīrtayanto mām*—always chant My glories' (9.14).

> Kirtana is a way to appreciate the Lord, develop love for Him, express love towards Him and even experience His love.

The rhythmic chanting and musical elements can trigger a relaxing response in the body, promoting a sense of tranquillity. This can be particularly beneficial for individuals dealing with the stresses of daily life. *Kirtana* often involves expressing deep emotions through music. Participants sing with heartfelt devotion, allowing them to vent long-standing emotions and connect with their innermost feelings. This emotional release can be therapeutic and contribute to emotional well-being. Further, *sankirtana* is a communal activity where people come together to sing and chant. This shared spiritual experience can foster loving relationships with God at the centre.

Bhajana—A Plea for Service

Bhaj means 'a plea to serve'. *Bhajana* is a heartfelt appeal made by a soul seeking shelter in the sincere service of God, the Supreme Soul.

Bhajana is a prayer of a devotee expressing an eagerness to serve the Lord unconditionally. *Bhajana* can be a song that expresses one's heartfelt feelings and emotions, which has a tremendous soothing effect on the mind and it facilitates the absorption of one's mind in the devotional service of the Lord.

These appeals, in the form of devotional songs, are sung by great saints and spiritual musicians in appealing

melodies to inspire spiritual seekers. Devotional music takes on various forms and styles, reflecting our cultural diversity. Whether they are the soulful classical renditions in Carnatic or Hindustani music, the rhythmic and melodic patterns in *bhajanas*, or the energetic call-and-response singing in *kirtanas*, spiritual music caters to different tastes and preferences.

Prarthana—A Humble Prayer

Prarthana means 'prayer' or 'supplication' that expresses one's earnest and heartfelt wishes, requests or devotion to the Divine.

Prarthana can take various forms, including reciting specific prayers or *mantras*, offering praises and seeking blessings or guidance. It is an integral part of spiritual practices, seeking the Lord's protection and blessings, or expressing one's humble position before the Lord, gratitude for all the blessings received, apologies for the mistakes committed, asking for assistance in various aspects of life and other such spiritual sentiments. *Prarthana* can be a personal prayer to the Lord, or involve singing standard prayers composed by great saints.

Dhyana—A Deep Meditation

Dhyana means 'meditation', which refers to any form of deep thinking.

For example, you may read a book and literally enter into a state of absorption. This can be called your meditation on the book. But in a deeper sense, *dhyana* or

meditation refers to the process of raising our mind from lower levels to higher levels—or from inferior thoughts and desires to noble thoughts and desires. It is like climbing the stairs of a building to go from a lower floor to a higher floor where you get a wonderful view from the window. The process may seem exhausting, but the end result is exciting. Lord Krishna dedicates the entire sixth chapter of the Bhagavad-Gita to describe *dhyana-yoga* or the process of linking with the Supreme through mindful meditation. He concludes the chapter saying that one who constantly meditates on Him within one's heart with love and devotion is the best yogi. In the spiritual context, *dhyana* can take multiple forms:

1. *Nama-dhyana:* Meditating on the spiritual names of God
2. *Rupa-dhyana:* Meditating on the divine forms of God
3. *Guna-dhyana:* Meditating on the enchanting qualities of God
4. *Lila-dhyana:* Meditating on the amazing activities of God

Mantra meditation is the process of repeatedly focusing on one *mantra* for a long time. Of all the types of meditation, *mantra* meditation is the simplest and easiest. In one sense, this is called *japa*.

Japa—Private Chanting

Japa is the process of repeatedly 'uttering' a *mantra* or a sacred name of God a specific number of times daily.

A sound, word or a phrase, when repeated, can have a calming, soothing and transformative effect on the mind. When we only 'think' of a *mantra* within our mind, we may sometimes get diverted to other thoughts. So, great saints advised us to utter the *mantra* in a soft voice so that we can hear it with our ears. *Japa* involves 'hearing' the *mantra* that we are 'uttering', while 'counting' how many times we are uttering it on beads (*japa mala*). While the ears are attentively listening, the mouth is sincerely chanting and the hands are carefully counting the *mantras*, the unnecessary thoughts in the mind subside, distractions are controlled and we make a connection with the Divine Lord.

Japa is a kind of sacrifice. A sacrifice is not just a fire sacrifice but any noble endeavour taken up for a virtuous purpose. Lord Krishna says in the Gita: '*yajñānām japa-yajño 'smi*—Of all the sacrifices, I am the process of chanting the names of God' (10.25).

A Pause for Prayer

All the above forms of spiritual practices that involve thinking, uttering or singing the names, forms, qualities and activities of God in a humble mood of prayer have a tremendous positive impact on our mind and overall well-being.

Whether you are chanting a *mantra*, singing a devotional song privately or congregationally, reciting a set of *shlokas* or meditating on a particular quality of God, a sincere, prayerful mood is the foundational principle of spiritual music. And the purpose of this enlivening

spiritual activity is to ultimately connect with the Divine Lord. When we are situated in this consciousness, then we will also be given access to the free gifts and by-products of spiritual music in the form of relaxation, de-stressing, emotional regulation and a sense of unity. Initially, one may look for the by-products, but we will benefit greatly by aiming for the ultimate purpose.

Singing Like a Donkey

The mighty warrior Arjuna was great at music. Once, his elder brother Bhima, known for his great physical strength, also developed a desire to become an expert musician like Arjuna. He approached a music teacher, took some lessons and started practising loudly near their royal palace at Indraprastha. Hearing the earth-shattering sounds, some citizens gently complained to King Yudhishthira about the disturbance caused by Bhima's loud singing.

King Yudhishthira then requested Draupadi to speak to Bhima. Draupadi then told Bhima, 'Music is a very specialized skill blessed upon a godly few. Please shift to a secluded mountainous forest region nearby, to expedite your musical proficiency.' Bhima liked Draupadi's suggestion and shifted to a nearby forest on a mountain and continued his diligent music practice.

One day, a villager saw Bhima from the bushes. With a startled look on his face, he started running away. Bhima became suspicious and started chasing the man. Bhima finally caught him and asked, 'Who are you? Why did you start running away upon seeing me?'

The villager, shaking like a leaf in Bhima's grip, replied, 'I am a washerman in this village. I had lost one of my donkeys. When I heard your voice, I thought I had found my donkey. With great joy I came to the spot, only to find that it was your voice!'

Bhima became morose on hearing this and retired from his music practice.

After a few days, Yudhishthira asked Bhima to bring Lord Krishna from Dwaraka. Bhima planned to set out for Dwaraka after breakfast, but he decided to rest for a while before departing. As Bhima lay down, he heard a loud knock on his door. Bhima got up and opened it.

Yudhishthira was standing at the door. He said, 'Bhima, I told you to bring Lord Krishna here, but you slept till afternoon and still didn't leave from here.' Annoyed, Yudhishthira departed and Bhima felt ashamed for not fulfilling the small request of his elder brother.

In deep regret, Bhima closed the door and cried out for forgiveness from Lord Krishna, acknowledging his mistake. He prayed with humility, 'O Krishna! O Vasudeva! O Dwarakadhisha! O Bhaktavatsala! O Acyuta! O Keshava! O Damodara! I don't have much time now. Please empower me to fulfil Yudhishthira's order despite the limited time.'

While Bhima thus fervently prayed to Lord Krishna, he heard another knock on his door. Yudhishthira stood there, smiling and appreciating Bhima. 'Bhima, you are so humble that you never told me that you have already brought Lord Krishna from Dwaraka before noon.'

Bhima saw Lord Krishna behind Yudhishthira and was surprised.

Seeing Bhima confused, Lord Krishna later embraced him and said, 'Dear Bhima, your heartfelt prayer brought Me here. I was not so impressed with your musical practice in the secluded forest, but I am attracted to your humble calling out of My names when Yudhishthira scolded you.' Bhima was overwhelmed and fell at Lord Krishna's feet, bathing them with his tears of gratitude.

This is the power of heartfelt prayer. The power of spiritual music originating from the heart appeals to the Lord more than the music generated from instruments and speakers. Nevertheless, those who are blessed with the ability to sing well and play instruments well can use all those skills in their prayers and thus inspire others too.

What Does Spiritual Music Do?

Spiritual music is for those who want to uplift their consciousness to heights untouchable by worldly distresses and pains. It has a remarkable ability to swiftly generate a revolution of positivity and peace in our hearts.

Many devotional songs draw inspiration from scriptures, including the Vedas, Upanishads, Puranas, Bhagavad-Gita and Bhagavatam. The lyrics often convey philosophical teachings, moral values and narratives from spiritual texts, serving as a medium for both education and inspiration.

Devotional music is considered a powerful tool for spiritual upliftment. It helps individuals connect with the

Divine, transcend worldly concerns and experience a sense of inner peace and bliss. The repetitive chanting of *mantras* and singing of devotional songs are believed to have a purifying and transformative effect on the mind and soul.

Also, devotional music plays a role in preserving and transmitting cultural traditions from generation to generation. The oral tradition of passing down devotional songs has been a crucial aspect of maintaining spiritual culture.

Spiritual music calms the mind. Apart from singing and music, we can cultivate the habit of personal chanting or *japa*. Repeatedly chanting a *mantra* is a traditional, spiritual and meditative practice. Make it a practice to chant a *mantra* for at least a few minutes in a day, while trying to pull the mind back from all distractions. Just like a shield, these *mantras*, when chanted attentively, will protect you from all sorts of distractions.

Spiritual music, prayer and *japa* improve concentration. Repetitive chanting helps us focus our mind on a single sound vibration. This concentration practice can enhance our attention span and improve our ability to stay focused and mindful throughout the day. With increased levels of concentration and mindfulness, we can be more productive in our work and relationships and make spiritual advancement as well. Managing our emotions also becomes easier.

When you chant the Almighty Lord's names, for example, 'Vasudeva', 'Krishna', 'Rama', 'Narayana' and so on, you naturally feel a sense of connection with Him. Such emotional bonding with the Lord through chanting

His names will surely help you manage your emotions well. You will be able to see yourself guided by Him from within. The more you chant and meditate on His name, the more you can maintain your calm even amidst chaotic circumstances.

The rhythmic repetition of *mantras* can stimulate the brain and improve memory retention. This can be beneficial for academic learning and focused study.

A Mantra to Calm Your Mind

There are unlimited *mantras* mentioned in the timeless scriptures. These *mantras* typically contain the names of the Supreme Almighty Lord, the Supreme Father, protector and maintainer of all living beings. We are all His eternal children. In this way, *mantras* are an effective way to connect with Him. Here is a simple, sweet and effective *mantra* to chant privately or congregationally sing every day. This is called the '*maha mantra*' or the great *mantra*, specifically recommended in the scriptures for this age.

> *'Hare Krishna Hare Krishna Krishna Krishna Hare Hare*
> *Hare Rama Hare Rama Rama Rama Hare Hare'*

This *mantra* has only sixteen words, in which only three words are repeated. So, it's very easy to chant. Try chanting it lovingly. Just like an elevator has a powerful force (electricity) that helps it go up quickly, the Hare Krishna *maha mantra*'s potency lifts our thoughts and feelings. It unlocks a door that leads to a place of joy and good thoughts, and ultimately a sweet relationship with Lord Krishna, the speaker of the Gita.

Practices for Inner Balance

1. *Sing Devotionally:* If you have musical abilities, use them in your prayers to inspire others. Listen to or engage in spiritual music to uplift your consciousness and bring positivity and peace into your heart.
2. *Pray Heartily:* Engage in heartfelt prayers to the Divine, focusing on sincerity and emotional connection rather than doing it as a ritual or just a musical performance.
3. *Connect with Spiritual Texts:* Explore devotional songs inspired by spiritual scriptures. Reflect on the philosophical teachings, moral values and narratives conveyed in the lyrics.
4. *Cultivate Personal Chanting:* Develop a daily habit of *japa* with a *mantra* for at least a few minutes attentively, and pull the mind back from distractions by focusing it on a single sound vibration.
5. *Emotional Management:* Chant the names of the Almighty Lord to foster a sense of connection and emotional bonding, and thus maintain calmness in chaotic circumstances.
6. *Preserve Culture:* Recognize the role of devotional music in preserving and transmitting cultural traditions. Contribute to the oral tradition by sharing devotional songs with others, and promote congregational singing of devotional songs for a collective spiritual experience.

16

When a Dear One Departs

Practical Insights into Coping with Death

One of my friends, an esteemed scientist in a popular organization, is very intelligent, active and a quick learner. He is well-versed with material sciences and spiritual philosophy. He is well-read in wisdom texts like the Bhagavad-Gita. He is a good speaker, manager, organizer, achiever and an experienced, rational thinker. His questions during our spiritual discussions were always very pertinent, logical and philosophical. I don't remember hearing him say anything superficial or sentimental.

One day, I received a phone call from him. I answered the call and heard his voice faltering due to deep emotions. With tears in his eyes, he informed me that his mother passed away due to some illness that she had been suffering from for a long time. He was extremely emotional, and his tears depicted a trait completely opposite to his

philosophical persona. I expressed my condolences and tried to console him. I spoke to his family and friends, and offered whatever little assistance I could.

Many weeks later, he sent me a long text in which he mentioned that he was unable to come out of the trauma of his mother's death. He was crying in guilt and pain every day, and his family was unable to help him control his emotions and tears. He was unable to focus on his work.

I was a bit surprised and concerned that such a wise and philosophical person was so overwhelmed for such a long time. I acknowledged his emotions and tried to pacify him in many ways. Certainly, his intelligence was able to understand the truth, but his emotions were unable to digest the fact. The same is the case with most people, including scholars, philosophers and spiritualists on the planet, and I consider myself to be no exception.

> *Our philosophical understanding doesn't, needn't and shouldn't kill our emotions!*

Let's dive deep into the interplay of the rational and emotional faculties in our being and understand whether we should resolve the conflict between our philosophical capabilities and fine sentiments, from the standpoint of the Gita.

Our Rational and Emotional Sides

Oftentimes, we tend to think that discretion and emotion move in opposite directions. This is the case

with most individuals. Some people may be predominantly rational, but they do have emotions. Others may be predominantly emotional; still, they too have some logic and reasoning.

All of us have both mind and intelligence within our subtle bodies. The mind is the emotional faculty and intelligence is the rational one. While the mind is a storehouse of desires, feelings and emotions, the role of intelligence includes discernment, analysis, logic and reasoning. While intelligence helps us to philosophically reconcile a situation, the mind tends to overwhelm us with feelings, thoughts, desires, attachments and aversions. In this inner battle, the victory of one of these faculties depends on the time, place, person and the situation at hand.

Let's consider an example to make things clearer.

Assume our mind desires to have a fried delicacy, but our intelligence knows that fried items are not good for health. So, there is a struggle going on within us. If our mind overpowers our intelligence, we will have the dish, but if our intelligence emerges triumphant, we shall refrain from doing so.

This simple and innocent scenario repeats in much graver situations of life where we take vital life decisions either after thorough analysis by the intelligence or instigated by deep emotions and sentiments of the mind.

Doesn't it seem that a decision or an action based on diligent intelligence is better than that which is driven by the mind's emotions? Well, not necessarily. Both have their crucial role to play in our lives.

The effectiveness of our decisions and actions depends on how well we balance our rational and emotional sides.

Let's analyse the example of Arjuna from the Bhagavad-Gita to understand this better.

Arjuna's Inner Battle

In the profound opening of the Bhagavad-Gita, Arjuna, torn between duty and compassion, found himself at a crossroads. Although all formalities were done and dusted, and it was time for actual business, the moment Arjuna took up his bow and was ready to shoot, he suddenly asked Lord Krishna, 'Please draw my chariot in the centre of both the armies. I wish to see who wants to fight me.'

Weren't there intense strategic meetings held by the Pandavas before the battle? Didn't Arjuna know who he was going to lock horns with? Definitely, Arjuna knew all those who stood opposite him in the battlefield. But still, he wasn't convinced at heart. Arjuna was looking forward to peacemaking, but forced by the obstinacy of Duryodhana, he had agreed to fight.

In this world, we are not always free to act according to our own choices but are obliged to respond to others' moods, deeds and needs—either positive or negative.

But the prospect of slaying loved ones, teachers and revered elders weighed heavily on his conscience. He questioned the purpose of the war, contemplating the emptiness

victory might bring without the cherished presence of family members.

Amidst the chaos of the battlefield, Arjuna, burdened by conflicting emotions, stood with bow in hand, hesitant to be violent upon his own kin. The air was thick with tension as he gazed at familiar faces turned foes. Bhishma, Drona and countless relatives stood ready for battle.

This introspective pause reflected Arjuna's indecisiveness and inner battle between his rational and emotional faculties, between his sense of duty and morality. While facing the brunt of the harsh reality of war, Arjuna sought clarity in the face of moral ambiguity.

Lord Krishna immediately agreed to Arjuna's request. Right there, Arjuna saw his teachers, grandfathers, uncles, sons, brothers and friends, all ready to fight. Overwhelmed with sympathy, Arjuna presented various reasons to not fight. He wanted to forget and forgive all the heinous crimes of the Kauravas—poisoning Bhima, setting their house on fire, attempting to disrobe Draupadi, usurping their kingdom by playing a rigged gambling match.

An action that lacks conviction doesn't sustain for too long.

Lord Krishna's Logical Perspectives

Arjuna was confused and presented several arguments showcasing why he shouldn't be fighting. But Lord Krishna reset his emotions with His rational perspectives, especially the science of the soul and body.

He said, 'My dear Arjuna, you are lamenting unnecessarily. Don't think that you will literally be able to kill all your relatives. Your arrows will only be piercing their bodies, but the person within the body, the soul, is eternal. The material body is just a covering on the spirit soul.'

dehino 'smin yathā dehe
kaumāraṁ yauvanaṁ jarā
tathā dehāntara-prāptir
dhīras tatra na muhyati

'Even within one life, the embodied soul continuously passes in this body from boyhood to youth to old age. Similarly, the soul passes into another body at the time of death. So, one should never be bewildered by such a change' (BG 2.13).

Lord Krishna then inspired Arjuna to look at the situation from a positive perspective. 'In fact, you should rejoice in the changes of the body, as one gets a new body with rejuvenated energy. Because Bhishma and Drona are noble souls, they will surely get spiritual bodies or, at least, heavenly bodies. In either case, there is no need for you to lament. The eternal spirit soul is indestructible and imperishable, and its existence is beyond the birth and death of the body' (BG 2.16–21).

No one can save the body from death, and no one can kill the eternal soul.

To make it easy for Arjuna to understand, Lord Krishna provided a simple analogy.

vāsāmsi jīrṇāni yathā vihāya
navāni gṛhṇāti naro 'parāṇi
tathā śarīrāṇi vihāya jīrṇāny
anyāni samyāti navāni dehī

'Just as a person gives up old garments and accepts new ones, similarly, the soul gives up old and useless bodies and attains new bodies' (BG 2.22).

Inspiring Arjuna to not ignore his duty as a warrior prince to protect virtue and fight against vice in the form of Duryodhana, Lord Krishna said, 'The soul cannot be cut by weapons, burnt by fire, moistened by water or withered by wind. You may have weapons made of all these elements, but none of these weapons can destroy the soul. The soul is unbreakable, insoluble, everlasting and unchangeable. One who is born is destined to die, and after death, rebirth is inevitable. Both birth and death are unavoidable. Therefore, all you need to fulfil is your duty of fighting the war. Do not lament for the perishable bodies of your relatives. Even if you don't kill them in this battle, they will die in another battle. Even if they don't participate in any other battle, by nature's law, they will surely die one day, when their bodies dwindle or decay out of disease. But if you shy away from your duty of fighting, you will incur the sin of being irresponsible' (BG 2.23–25, 31–36).

It is only due to the presence of the soul that the body is animated, otherwise the body is just a combination of perishable material elements that are subject to constant transformations and deteriorations. Undue attachment for

temporary bodily relationships puts one in confusion, fear and loss of mental equilibrium.

The soul is ever alive, and the body is never alive.

Hearing such a logical, deep and insightful explanation from Lord Krishna about the body and soul, and many other such philosophical subjects in the Gita, Arjuna was convinced and donned his armour once again. But there was a surprise awaiting Arjuna and unfortunately for him, it was an unpleasant one!

Strong Emotions despite Deep Insights

During the Kurukshetra war, amidst the battle, Arjuna's beloved son Abhimanyu was unjustly attacked by several senior warriors on Duryodhana's side. Upon learning of Abhimanyu's death, Arjuna, overwhelmed by emotions, tears and anger, vowed to avenge his son before sunset the next day or end his own life by entering fire, even in the presence of Lord Krishna.

Arjuna's intense emotional response may seem contradictory to the philosophical teachings imparted by Lord Krishna in the Bhagavad-Gita just before the war. Lord Krishna never told Arjuna, 'Did you forget what I explained about the eternal nature of the soul and the temporary nature of the body? Why are you getting so emotional about Abhimanyu's death? Just focus on the war!' Instead, Lord Krishna stayed with Arjuna, acknowledged Arjuna's emotions and got his back.

The apparent contradiction indicates that philosophical insights do not and should not suppress emotions. While a wise person comprehends the temporary nature of material relationships, it doesn't mean emotions towards these relationships should be devoid of sensitivity, love, care, concern and kindness. The body's impermanence doesn't negate the importance of being compassionate, caring and responsible in our connections.

A wise individual mourns the death of a loved one not out of ignorance but because they miss the inspiring association of the departed. One shouldn't become dysfunctional in grief but rather cherish memories, feel the departed's presence through those memories and continue to be a well-wisher to others.

Understanding the temporary nature of material existence doesn't preclude feeling for others' pain. Compassion, kindness and extending a helping hand are essential aspects of being human, what to speak of being spiritual. Despite life's impermanence, cherished moments, memories and the impact of meaningful interactions can endure beyond death.

While feeling emotions is natural and human, dwelling in a dysfunctional state indefinitely isn't advisable. Acceptance, digestion and moving forward in life are crucial. However, this doesn't mean becoming cold and emotionless; after all, emotions distinguish living beings from dead matter.

In essence, it's about striking a balance between acknowledging life's impermanence, feeling deeply and yet maintaining emotional resilience and functionality.

Being wise doesn't mean lacking emotion, having emotions doesn't mean we are foolish.

Balancing Discretion and Emotion

Before the war, when Arjuna's emotional turmoil over his relatives on Duryodhana's side overshadow his commitment to the war, Lord Krishna discouraged Arjuna from being excessively emotional or sentimental. However, when Arjuna was grief-stricken at Abhimanyu's tragic death, Lord Krishna didn't suppress Arjuna's emotions, but opted to assist him in finding composure. Why did Lord Krishna behave in an apparently contradictory manner?

Arjuna's emotional states before the war and during the Kurukshetra war after his son's death reveal two significant distinctions.

1. Firstly, Arjuna's pre-war emotions were misplaced and entangled with his relatives on Duryodhana's side, who had chosen the path of *adharma* (vice), and thus they lacked justification. In contrast, his post-Abhimanyu emotions, as a grieving father, were justified, considering Abhimanyu's virtuous character and Arjuna's natural fatherly affection.
2. The second disparity lies in Arjuna's response to duty. Before the war, he contemplated abandoning his role as a warrior, driven by emotional turmoil. However, after Abhimanyu's death, Arjuna did not shun his duty but vowed to teach a lesson to those responsible for his son's unjust killing. His commitment to duty, even in the face of personal

tragedy, reflected a fierce warrior spirit without compromising his sense of duty.

Beyond these differences, delving into the intricacies of emotions reveals their dual nature. While emotions like love, compassion, kindness and gratitude enrich our lives and relationships, these very emotions, when misdirected or irrationally applied towards undeserving individuals, can lead to harm.

Cultivating emotional resilience requires rational intelligence to discern the validity of emotions.

Intelligence, as the regulating faculty of the mind's thoughts, desires, feelings and emotions, should actively analyse whether these mental aspects are justified or not. Striking a balance between wisdom and emotion enhances the journey of life, ensuring a more meaningful and vibrant existence.

What Can I Do for the Departed?

To honour and maintain a soul-to-soul connection with our beloved who has passed away, the Vedic texts offer wisdom that guides us in meaningful practices, transcending bodily designations.

Amongst many such practices, offering heartfelt personal prayers to the Lord to bless the onward spiritual journey of the departed soul is considered most well-wishing. Such prayers protect the soul and offer it immense protection.

We can also participate in devotional activities and services on behalf of the departed one, contribute to noble causes and engage in selfless work in memory of the beloved, fostering a positive impact in their honour. Thus, by performing all these acts and praying to the Lord to keep our beloved in His shelter, we can serve and maintain a connection with our dear ones even after they are gone.

Practices for Inner Balance

1. *Balance Decisions with Discretion and Emotion:* Wisely analyse and ensure a balance between the logical and emotional aspects of a situation before making important life decisions.
2. *Accept and Move On:* Recognize life's impermanence and the inevitability of change, and don't get stuck in your duties by being overly emotional or sentimental. Yet, don't be emotionally insensitive.
3. *Strike a Balance:* Embrace emotions as a vital aspect of being human, without compromising on rationality and responsibilities. Apply the wisdom gained from philosophical insights to daily life situations.
4. *Cultivate Emotional Resilience:* Validate your emotions through rational intelligence, by acknowledging the dual nature of emotions—enriching when directed properly, potentially harmful when misdirected.
5. *Honouring Departed Loved Ones:* Offer personal prayers, express love, gratitude and positive wishes for departed loved ones.

Practices for Inner Balance

17

So Much Pain—'Why Me?!'

A Journey from Anguish to Awakening

Once, a bee started sipping the nectar inside a lotus flower. Evening was approaching, but the sweet intoxicating nectar had left it oblivious to the fast-approaching sunset. With the sun dropping below the horizon, the lotus petals began to close. Soon the bee found itself trapped inside the flower. With no escape route available, the helpless bee collapsed forever.

Who do you think was responsible for the bee's death? The lotus or the sun?

While the honey inside the lotus gave the bee enjoyment, the petals of the lotus caused the bee's death. But the lotus itself was neither attached nor averse to the bee. As far as the sun is concerned, the sun just follows its routine of rising and setting while giving the same heat and light to everybody. It is not partial or inimical

towards anyone. The reason for the bee's death is that the bee didn't buzz off at the right time!

The joys and sorrows of life are results of our own good or bad deeds, technically called karma. Knowing this can help relieve us of the 'pointing fingers' disease.

This lesson seems logical and clear in the case of the bee, because both the lotus and the sun were neutral. But what about us? Is *karma* the cause of every kind of misery that we face? Aren't there some nefarious people who take pleasure in troubling the innocent? What is the reason for their suffering? Again, *karma*? Doesn't the culprit have any role apart from being an instrument in the hands of the victim's *karma*?

I had such questions and in my interactions with various people, I encountered such questions. Now let's dig into the answers and the complex dynamics of *karma*, based on the teachings of the Gita and other wisdom texts. And I promise you, this is going to be far from textual!

The Painful Duo

The timeless texts inform us that in this world we face three types of pains.

1. *Personal Pain:* Pains caused by one's own body and mind—like health issues, mental confusion and so on.
2. *Natural Pain:* Pains caused by seasonal changes and natural calamities like excessive rain, summer heat, winter cold, etc.

3. *Induced Pain:* Pains caused by other living beings, like people around us, or even animals and insects.

All these pains are difficult pills to swallow, and this is where we need to understand the law of *karma*. Let's present the types of pain in two categories from the perspective of visible and invisible human sources of pain.

1. *Who's the Culprit?* These are situations when we face hardships and pain and undergo trauma as a result of the actions of people with wicked intentions.
2. *Karma's the Culprit?* This is a scenario where we have no one deliberately acting against us, and we put in all the endeavours and even garner support from our well-wishers, but in the end, we find ourselves flowing down the drain.

Now, since we have both the causes of unfavourable circumstances before us, let's get to broadening our understanding of both of them.

In life, people around us may sometimes act as heroes, villains or neutral parties. Their hero avatars may be welcomed and neutral demeanours may be accepted, but the problem is when they put on their dark side. The tapestry of their villainy may produce fallbacks, failures and other such obstacles in our life. The most painful part is that these impediments are not simply happenstance. In fact, they are calculated, well-planned actions born out of malice. The Pandavas were a vivid example of this case. Once, the tyrannical Duryodhana poisoned Bhima.

Later, he tried burning all the Pandavas and their mother Kunti in a house made of lac by employing someone to set it ablaze. Next, he cheated the Pandavas in a gambling match, eventually usurping their kingdom. But worst of all, he tried disrobing Draupadi, the chaste wife of the Pandavas, openly in public. Of course, their beloved Lord Krishna intervened and protected Draupadi's honour by manifesting as a mystical sari. These were only a few of the traumatizing events that Duryodhana played out against the five brothers.

But sometimes it so happens that we find all the support we need, add in all the effort and have no enemy, but despite this, all we encounter is a downfall. The cause at times is an unforeseen event or an external factor beyond our control. This is where helplessness kicks into our life. Examples of such a scenario could be getting late to work because of an unanticipated earthquake. An unexpected road closure, accident, a seasonal change or a natural calamity could have similar outcomes.

Depending on the intensity of pain caused by the aforementioned sources, common reactions could be:

1. *For the pain caused by a visible culprit:* Blaming, blaspheming, grudging and developing negativity towards those who threw obstacles across our path.
2. *For the pain caused by unseen forces:* Blaming God, destiny, our own fortune; or getting disappointed, depressed, demotivated, discouraged and dysfunctional may be our natural reaction.

But now is the time to change our responses by performing a deep scan of whichever situation we are currently in. And how do we do that?

Let's unravel this together.

Am I (Not) Responsible?

The foremost aspect of a refined response to any kind of misery is to check if there is any mistake on one's own part, and if so, quickly acknowledge, rectify and make sure one does not repeat it.

> *Denying personal responsibility for one's pain only perpetuates the pain!*

But for every me and you, it would be natural to identify a cause beyond ourselves. The reason is simple—no one desires suffering, and generally, no sensible person performs any action with an intention to suffer. Desiring and endeavouring for pleasure and attempting to avoid pain are natural for all living beings. Oftentimes, however, we don't get the joys we expect and we can't escape the sorrows we dread. When our seamless plans lead to tragic results, when our good deeds performed with integrity end in turmoil, we naturally feel confused and disappointed. It is in such situations that we tend to blame others, who seem to be the immediate cause of our predicament.

'I am suffering because of him!' 'The pain I'm experiencing is because of her!' 'Had this event not

occurred, I would have been happier today!' How many times have these thoughts or statements entered our mind or ears?

We often hear that we reap the results of our own actions, i.e., the pleasant and unpleasant experiences in our life are consequences of our own deeds. Many people accept that idea, but inconsistently. They tend to take credit for their success and conveniently believe that their happiness is due to their own good work. But when their actions produce unintended results, they think to themselves, 'Am I really suffering due to my own actions? How can it be?'

> *It requires courage and honesty to accept responsibility for one's failures and pains. Blaming others for one's suffering is easy.*

Although the symptoms of a disease indicate the immediate cause, an expert physician traces out the root cause. A painkiller may relieve the immediate physical pain, but proper diagnosis and medication are needed to fully cure the patient. Likewise, a mature person tries to identify the cause behind the immediate cause, and thus traces out the root cause of one's failure and misery.

Understanding the Law of Karma

The term *karma* basically means 'action', but it is also used to indicate a 'reaction' or the result of an action, or the whole cycle of actions and reactions. Good actions lead to pleasant results, and bad actions lead to bad consequences. Sometimes, the reactions to our actions come instantly and sometimes they are delayed, but they certainly come.

This is called the law of *karma*. Just like a state or national government frames certain laws, the universal government has the law of *karma*, as ordained by God, the ultimate authority.

In accordance with the law of *karma*, we receive bad reactions to our bad actions *through* various people, and thinking that we received troubles *from* them, we tend to blame them as the cause of our suffering, or unwittingly blame God for our distress. But the real cause of our suffering is our own misdeeds. The veil of emotions in distressing situations bewilders most people who then fail to use this simple logic.

To reconcile tricky situations, use discretion, not emotion.

The law of *karma* works in amazing ways. Let's say I deserve to suffer a reaction due to my past bad *karma*. Now, I may receive that reaction *through* someone who may have a tendency to act inappropriately. By acting as an instrument of my *karma*, that person may incur some *karma* as well and receive his *karmic* reaction through someone else. The Lord is the creator of this system of *karma*—or actions and reactions. By His omnipotence, in this humungous network of *karmas* of innumerable individuals, people come together and are separated, thereby experiencing their individual *karmas* through each other in various situations. We may or may not be aware of whom we troubled or those whom we troubled! But the pleasant and unpleasant material experiences are inevitable as long as one holds on to a *karmic* baggage of various actions and reactions.

Instead of hating a miscreant who directly inflicts suffering upon them, wise people identify their own deeds as the cause of their suffering.

Should I (Not) Avoid Misery?

'I agree that I am suffering due to my misdeeds, and its coming *through* a miscreant, and not *from* him, but what about his misdeed?' If this is your question, the answer is: 'The person who misused his freedom to act and caused you pain shall also suffer surely.'

You may now ask, 'Should I just understand that he will suffer for his *karma* and keep quiet? Should I not take action against him?'

The answer is . . .

Yes! You must certainly take appropriate action. And that's what Lord Krishna taught Arjuna. Arjuna wasn't expected to keep quiet, thinking that it was due to his *karma* that they faced difficulties 'through' Duryodhana. Lord Krishna encouraged Arjuna to fight for justice, and not tolerate injustice, thinking that the law of *karma* is at play.

Misery is inevitable, but not unavoidable.

In the monsoon season, showers are common almost everywhere, but does it mean that we don't pull out our umbrellas? By all means, we need to avoid being drenched as much as possible. While living in this world, one should be intelligent enough to avoid suffering as much as humanly possible, and if the suffering exceeds one's

capacity, one has to accept the inevitable as God's will and a result of one's past deeds.

One may have to tolerate suffering that comes of its own accord, but one shouldn't allow oneself to be exploited unnecessarily.

Why Suffer More than You Deserve?

However, we may sometimes suffer more than necessary by holding grudges, carrying negative impressions, making biased decisions, dealing with people based on conceptions and perceptions born of our suffering and so on. All this leads to unnecessary suffering that we unconsciously inflict upon ourselves and others.

Being caught up in dealing with the immediate or intermediate causes of suffering creates more suffering through various channels, namely, the blame game, imagination, overthinking, gossip and negative propaganda. Blaming inspires others to blame, and this contagious blame game can expand to multiple people for a long time and create more suffering and agitation in the minds of those involved. Therefore, responsibly addressing the cause of suffering while keeping negativity at bay would be a sensible thing to do. And that's exactly what the Pandavas did in the battle at Kurukshetra.

Although Duryodhana hated Yudhishthira, Yudhishthira never hated Duryodhana, although he was supposed to fight Duryodhana. It was due to Duryodhana's whimsical actions that the Pandavas needed to responsibly teach him

a lesson but all of this without the slightest tinge of hatred in their hearts.

> *A mature person externally addresses the situation with responsibility while internally reconciling it as karma sanctioned by the Supreme will.*

A wrong has to be rectified. But rectification is not a channel to vent revenge. However, it is a responsibility that entails compassion even towards the one who 'caused' the trouble.

> *Addressing the cause of suffering with tolerance, forgiveness, gratitude and dependence on God's will is liberating.*

In contrast to the suffering of common people, we see those who are not following a spiritual path or even basic moral codes enjoy a life of prosperity. What is the reason for that? How does the law of *karma* work there?

Why Do Good Things Happen to Bad People?

Often, people pose this question: 'It's evident that some individuals are sinful, exploitative, selfish, greedy and even tyrannical, yet they find themselves in favourable material positions, enjoying fame and prosperity. If everyone has to face the consequences of their bad activities, why do these people, with so many negative qualities, make merry while several righteous people struggle for the bare necessities of life?'

The simple answer to this question is again the law of *karma*. During my BTech programme, I studied reasonably well and achieved good scores. This led me to a seat at the prestigious Indian Institute of Science (IISc) Bangalore, for my master's degree. This allowed me to enjoy the opulence of the IISc campus, with access to all its perks—fantastic classrooms, auditoriums, top-notch professors, labs, libraries, sports facilities, quality food at subsidized rates, excellent accommodation, a hefty scholarship and much more. The fee that my father had to pay for my master's was far lower than the stipend that I received. Overall, I was doing great.

At IISc, I continued with my BTech study habits but soon, I realized they were falling short of IISc standards. Honestly, I was also a little distracted by the new atmosphere and frequent outings with some relatives in the city. Naturally, my scores were not up to par in the first semester. Luckily, I didn't fail, but my scores were in bad shape and the reasons were evident. I felt awkward, and I intensified my study efforts in the second semester, resulting in significantly better scores.

Instead of improving my efforts, had I performed like I did in the first semester, I probably would have lost access to all those facilities and privileges I was enjoying at IISc.

Now let's go back the original question. I hope you would have got an answer to some extent by now. But still, here is a detailed explanation. People who are currently enjoying prosperity are reaping the results of their past good

activities. However, if they don't act properly now, they will inevitably face the consequences of their current bad activities in the future. The current happiness and prosperity are the results of their past good activities, and that good *karmic* credit will eventually exhaust, giving way to the repercussions of their current abominable actions. This is akin to someone who has earned a lot of money and is now spending it all for enjoyment, without endeavouring to earn more. Once they run out of their savings, they will return to square one—a state of financial hardship.

On the other hand, if those who are in an underprivileged condition exhibit good behaviour, refrain from sin and engage in positive actions, they exhaust the baggage of their past bad deeds and, in the future, are sure to experience the positive results of their current good nature and activities.

The word *random* can't be spelt randomly; how then can we assume that situations in our life come up randomly?

Another common question is: 'When I take to spirituality, the path of devotion or *bhakti*, does it destroy my *karma* or suffering? If that is true, then why do I find spiritualists, worshippers of God, suffering as well?'

Well, let's uncover the answer in the next chapter.

Practices for Inner Balance

1. *Take Responsibility for Your Mistakes:* Regularly reflect on and assess your actions, decisions and their consequences. If there are any mistakes on your part, promptly acknowledge and rectify them.
2. *Understand the Law of Karma*: Embrace the idea that both pleasant and unpleasant experiences in life are consequences of your own deeds—the cycle of actions and reactions.
3. *Avoid Extra Suffering*: Be mindful of how you respond to situations caused by visible culprits. Don't hold grudges, make biased decisions or engage in negative behaviours that create unnecessary pain.
4. *Address and Reconcile*: Take appropriate action against the wrongdoers without succumbing to revenge. Externally address the cause of suffering and internally reconcile it as *karma* sanctioned by a higher power.
5. *Tolerate, Forgive and Be Grateful*: Cultivate tolerance and forgiveness in the face of adversity, depend on a higher power's will and liberate yourself from negative emotions by promoting a positive mindset.

18

Can Spirituality Quash Misery?

A Deep Dive into the Capability of Spirituality

In the early years of my monkhood, there was a period when I was quite sick and was almost bedridden. I didn't have the strength to serve physically. During those days, the Bhagavad-Gita, spoken by Lord Krishna, and Srimad Bhagavatam, spoken about Lord Krishna, played vital roles as I struggled to recover. With each passing day, I delved deeper into scripture, drawing inspiration from stories that breathed devotion and non-textual philosophy.

One day, it so happened that my condition worsened. The doctor in our ashram advised me to visit a senior doctor in a hospital in Mumbai. It was a two-hour drive from the Ecovillage. I embarked on this curative journey. While on the way, I started losing my nerve. Why was this happening to me? At that point in time, I began praying.

Soon, I was at the hospital. I met the doctor and after conducting a thorough examination, he concluded there was nothing I needed to worry about. He put me on a diet, handed me some medicines and before saying goodbye, reassured me that everything would soon be all right. This simple act built in me a sense of comfort and relief. I swiftly travelled back to the ashram.

Upon entering my room, I reflected on my mindset during the journey. I was desperate and prayerful while going to the hospital. Surprisingly upon returning, I found I had left all that stress back in the car, and wasn't prayerful like before. A part of me felt ashamed upon realizing my contrasting emotions, while another part of myself was illuminated with a positive perspective and deep realization.

The first thought that made me ashamed was: 'It is in times of distress that we remember the Lord, but while in comfort, we generally forget Him.'

The second thought that enlivened me was: 'Calamities give us an opportunity to intensify our dependence on the Lord, and take us closer to Him. So, we shouldn't hate calamities; instead we can use them to strengthen our relationship with God.'

Calamities prompt intense remembrance of God, fostering dependence, whereas comfort tends to make us forget Him.

Whether in a happy or painful situation, an advanced spiritualist remembers the Lord with devotion during all peaks and troughs in life. I admitted to myself that

I wasn't advanced and had a long way to go on this path of spirituality.

> *An advanced spiritualist is one who maintains a prayerful connection with the Divine in both adversity and prosperity.*

But this leads to the fundamental question raised in the previous chapter: 'Why was I suffering sickness despite embracing a life of spiritual practice? Can't my *bhakti* relieve me from *karma*?'

I was someone who gave up my job, wealth, family comforts, varieties of garments and other such general privileges of a common man, and decided to dedicate my life in the service of God as a monk with a shaved head and saffron robes. Then why was I suffering? Can my beloved Lord Krishna not relieve my health issues? Should someone practising the spiritual life also encounter miseries due to *karma*?

Not just me, I know that many devotees, even senior members—both monks and householders—in our spiritual community are facing health issues, financial crunches and so on. All of this, despite their sincere and evolved practice of spiritual life for decades. The spiritual history of this universe reveals that even very elevated devotees of the Lord faced reversals. A vivid example is that of the Pandavas themselves, who underwent countless reversals, despite being fully devoted to Lord Krishna and having the Lord's intimate personal association.

Actually, many people approach God to get relief from suffering. This is what Lord Krishna said in the Gita (7.16)

as well. But why then does God not relieve their miseries? What is the purpose of following spirituality?

Can Bhakti Relieve Us from Karma?

In short, the answer is 'Yes! It can.'

The scripture Brahma Samhita boldly declares, '*karmāṇi nirdahati kintu ca bhakti-bhājām*'—*Bhakti* or sincere, loving, devotional service unto the Lord destroys all the reactions to one's material actions. Those who sincerely follow the spiritual path suffer not exactly due to their *karma*! Yes, you read it right. Let me elaborate.

Let's first look at the three types of people who face difficulties in this world:

1. Common people who do not follow any spiritual path, but just do their work honestly.
2. People who believe in God and follow spiritual practices of worshipping God, meditation, chanting his name and so on.
3. People who perfected their spiritual path and are already at the stage of self-realization and a loving relationship with God.

I am not adding sinful people to this list, because it is obvious that they deserve to suffer for their sinful and heinous deeds.

1. **Why Common People Suffer**

   People pursuing materialistic goals without any affiliation to spirituality suffer due to their *karma*. Even if someone strives to be as honest as

possible in this world, they surely tend to commit mistakes, even involuntarily, succumbing to many temptations. They may not intentionally harm others, or commit gravely sinful deeds, but sometimes their minds, distracted by the allurements of the world, often lead them to undesirable actions and reactions.

From simpler to more complex mistakes, whether it may be spending excessive time looking at the smartphone screen, overeating, oversleeping, indulging in sensual pleasures, being lazy at work or whatever, every faulty action results in a bad reaction and suffering, despite the absence of malicious intentions. The reasons for this suffering may be self-evident at times, but sometimes they might be unknown as well.

For instance, a pedestrian inadvertently steps on insects while walking, causing harm to smaller living beings. Perhaps someone deliberately kills innocent animals for consumption, gets intoxicated by alcohol, smokes cigarettes and expends their energy in sense enjoyment, thereby inviting inevitable suffering.

> *In the pursuit of pleasures in this world, one may unknowingly purchase pain at a heavy price due to unregulated habits and insane activities, and thus suffer the results of karma.*

2. Spirituality—A Zero-Suffering Guarantee?

Those who *practise* the spiritual path avoid all bad habits, including the consumption of intoxicants,

and also keep away from overindulgence in sense pleasures. At the same time, they embrace good habits like rising early, regulated work, worshipping, chanting the names of God, visiting temples, going on pilgrimage tours and associating with like-minded devotees. They maintain positivity, balance and regulation in their lifestyle and sincerely practise spirituality. In this way, they connect with God.

Why then should there be suffering in their lives?

The answer is—these people, being dedicated spiritualists, have their *karma* burnt in the fire of God's mercy. But still, as they advance from being a novice to an evolved stage, they had to deal with the traces of *anarthas* in them, and sometimes commit what is known as *aparadhas*.

- *Anarthas* refer to lingering unwanted desires, anger, envy, pride and greed. They persist during the initial phase of spirituality when one is not yet spiritually seasoned.
- *Aparadhas* refer to offences like inattention in spiritual practices, mistakes in worship, improper behaviour in holy places, disrespecting senior spiritualists and so on. These are committed due to flaws in spirituality.

Thus, practising spiritualists suffer not exactly due to their *karma* but due to the traces of *anarthas* and *aparadhas*. This suffering is personally orchestrated

by the Lord to rectify their erring tendencies and purify them of their shortcomings. Ultimately, divinity helps them grow in *bhakti*, perfecting their spiritual practice.

Just as a loving father or teacher may admonish or punish a child only for the child's betterment, similarly, the Lord gives token punishments to his practising devotees for their mistakes out of love. Eventually, these practising spiritualists turn into impeccable spiritualists and conquer all their shortcomings.

3. **Why Perfected Spiritualists Suffer**
   Spiritualists who have already perfected their *bhakti* face absolutely no *karmic* reactions due to their spiritually realized state. Yet, they encounter reversals in this world. Let me share some examples. The Pandavas were direct associates of Lord Krishna, intimately connected with Him. Still, they experienced hardships and troubles that Duryodhana and his camp had wickedly arranged. Kunti, the mother of the Pandavas, despite her devotion to Lord Krishna, also endured significant suffering. Prahlada, a famous child devotee, was targeted by his own father, Hiranyakashipu, the king of demons.

The Mystery of Misery

There are multiple reasons for the suffering of these perfected spiritualists.

Firstly, the Lord aims to highlight that, regardless of one's power, influence, devotion or purity, the nature of the world remains a place of suffering.

Secondly, the Lord wants to show this world that this suffering in the life of advanced spiritualists doesn't shake their faith. While immature devotees may lose their faith in God during adversity, mature devotees maintain an unshakeable faith in the intention and integrity of God despite life's challenges.

One who enjoys a relationship with God remains calm within, even amidst chaos outside.

The Lord allows suffering in their lives not out of His neglect towards them but to demonstrate how composed and satisfied one can be while in a whirlpool of chaos.

A mature spiritualist doesn't give up his/her faith and love for the Lord even in the midst of severe calamities.

Thirdly, suffering in this world enhances the pleasure in connection with God. The sunrise appears attractive because of the darkness of night. During the hot summer, cold water gives comfort; and during the cold winter, anything warm is pleasing. Lamplight appears attractive in darkness, not in the glaring light of day, and when one is distressed by hunger, even the most uninteresting dish tastes better than nectar. Similarly, the blissful appearance and activities of the Lord appear especially relishable after a brief phase of suffering.

Can I Be Suffering-Exempt?

Suffering is an intrinsic characteristic of this world. Imagine we're swimming in an ocean. Now, no matter how expertly we swim in the right direction, we're still going to get wet, isn't it? Similarly, this world is a place of suffering, because this is what its Creator has to say in the Bhagavad-Gita (8.15): '*dukhalayam ashasvatam*: This world is a place of misery and whatever happiness exists here is temporary.'

Think of a salt mine; whichever corner you go, you're sure to find only salt. Even by chance, it would be impossible to find sugar. Similarly, regardless of who we are, whatever may be our background, social status or education, challenges will come our way. Lord Krishna declares in the Gita (8.16) that the pain of birth, disease, old age and death are common for all embodied beings in all the planets of this universe—whether earth or hell or heaven or even the topmost planet of Lord Brahma.

The Gita's wisdom and the process of bhakti relieve us from the miseries of this world, not by literally eliminating the miseries but by enhancing our intellect with necessary wisdom to see a higher reason and purpose behind them.

> *Those who are on the spiritual path also encounter miseries, but they are not overwhelmed or unduly affected by them like common people.*

Understanding that suffering is sanctioned by the Lord for our rectification and purification, and learning to grow

through it instead of going through it, can help us rise above this world of suffering.

> *Spirituality doesn't stop the rains of distress but equips you with an umbrella.*

Overcoming suffering requires resilience, strategic thinking, devotion and a steadfast commitment to rising above the malevolence that seeks to deter us from our path. And this is the mystery of misery.

The additional benefit of spirituality is significant. Engaging in spiritual life not only diminishes past sins but also fortifies our mind with wisdom, reducing the inclination towards wrongful actions. It serves as a shield, safeguarding us not only from past transgressions but also preventing future sins by enhancing and spiritualizing our intelligence.

> *Spiritual life not only destroys the reactions to our past sins but also eradicates the sinning tendency by purifying our polluted intelligence.*

Practices for Inner Balance

1. *Be Prayerful:* Maintain a sincere connection with the Divine through regular prayer, worship, meditation and chanting, both in times of adversity and prosperity.
2. *Cultivate a Spiritual Lifestyle:* Embrace a life reflecting spiritual values, avoiding harmful indulgences like intoxicants and focusing on positive habits to strengthen your spiritual path.
3. *Avoid Anarthas and Aparadhas:* Recognize and eliminate lingering unwanted desires or *anarthas*, and avoid spiritual offences or *aparadhas* to grow in spiritual practice.
4. *Be Faithful:* Cultivate unwavering faith in the Divine, even amidst challenges, recognizing suffering as a natural part of the material world.
5. *Know the Purpose of Misery:* Embrace adversities, seeing them as opportunities for rectification, purification, spiritual growth and intensifying your connection with the Divine.

19

God's Fair Play

Contemporary Reflections on Divine Partiality

'Does God really exist? If so, is He really kind and equal to all? If yes, why are some people rich, some poor; some beautiful, some ugly; some suffer, some enjoy; some are educated, some illiterate? Why is there inequality and unhappiness in this world?'

These are some common questions I encountered in my travels and interactions with multiple audiences. In fact, at one point in time, even I had similar questions—not about the existence of God but about the disparity and misery in this world! A popular short story answered my question to some extent. Let me share it with you.

Once, a man went to a barber to get a haircut. While doing the trim, the barber said to the man, 'I don't think God exists; if He does, why is there so much suffering in

this world?' The man remained silent, and after the haircut was done, he left the salon.

After a while, he returned and said to the barber, 'I don't think barbers exist in this world!'

The barber was surprised and responded, 'I just gave you a haircut a while ago. Why then do you say so?'

The man replied, 'I see so many people wandering with long hair and beards! So, I concluded that there are no barbers in this world.'

The barber was amused. He said, 'They should come to me to get a haircut, and then can I give them a good shave too. Just because they have long hair and a thick beard doesn't mean that barbers don't exist!'

The man retorted, 'Exactly! Just because there are people suffering in this world doesn't mean God doesn't exist. They should approach God, worship Him and follow the prescribed spiritual practices!'

The barber learnt his lesson and so did I. But my next question was: 'Is God to be approached only during suffering? Do those who are happy need God? Why does this duality of happiness and suffering exist? Does it indicate the Lord's partiality?'

Honestly, reading the Bhagavad-Gita swept clean all those doubts. In fact, it left me with some invaluable learnings that I would love to share.

The Pain of Partiality

When parents are partial towards one child and neglect another, the latter would naturally be disappointed. When a teacher is partial towards one student, that would

inevitably discourage the other students. It is reasonable to expect from one's parents, teacher or elders similar treatment as one's equals receive. Any discrepancy in this leads to disappointment. Partiality is painful; it can demotivate people and slacken their spirits. Moreover, it can destroy people's faith in their elders or seniors and could even arouse rebellion. This is true even in the case of God.

Some happy people might ignore God while immersing themselves in enjoyment and material prosperity. Some may turn into disbelievers of God due to an intensely miserable experience in life. While the first category doesn't feel the need for God due to a sense of material security, the second category denies His existence, expecting Him to be a misery-reliever if He really existed. And there is a third category who, in their suffering, compare themselves with others, and say that God is partial, blaming Him for their unpleasant situations in life.

God is considered to be the eternal father, supreme teacher and the ultimate protector of all living beings, who are all His children, as Lord Krishna personally claims in the Gita: '*aham-bija-pradah pita*—I am the seed-giving father of all living beings. (14.4)' He also says, '*mama eva amsho jiva loke*—all the living beings are My fragmental parts' (15.7). Not just that, Lord Krishna says in the Gita (9.17-18) that He is the ultimate source, shelter, sustainer and well-wisher of everyone in the universe. There are many more such references, but let me present one more verse (9.29) here:

samo 'ham sarva-bhūteṣu
na me dveṣyo 'sti na priyah

Lord Krishna says in the Gita, 'I am equal to all. I envy no one, nor am I partial to anyone.'

If we are all His children, He is our supreme well-wisher, and if He is equal to everyone and is totally impartial, why should some of us suffer while others prosper? Does this disparity indicate a discrepancy in Lord Krishna's statements?

Is Favouritism Justified?

Consider the following example. A teacher in the classroom gives the same lecture to all the students without discrimination. But the attentive students are more eager to learn and approach the teacher with relevant inquiries on the subject. This pleases their teacher and he makes sure that he clarifies all the doubts his students have. On the other hand, the same teacher punishes a mischievous student. This is not the teacher's partiality or favouritism towards certain students but a natural response towards the students' behaviour.

Similarly, although the Lord is equal to everyone, He gives more attention to the virtuous. This favouritism is not a fault in Him; instead, it is a symbol of natural reciprocation. A careful study of the Gita reveals that the Lord is not literally *equal* to all, but He reciprocates with different people according to their mindsets and approach. Lord Krishna describes the threefold purpose of His various incarnations as:

1. To protect the virtuous
2. To punish the vicious
3. To establish righteousness

Instead of questioning why He protects some people and punishes others, asking ourselves 'Isn't it reasonable to deal with the virtuous and vicious in different ways?' may provide more clarity. Everyone agrees that such inequality is justified. This is Lord Krishna's reciprocal nature. He says, '*ye yatha mam prapadyante tams tathaiva bhajamy aham*—I reciprocate with people according to the mood in which they approach Me' (BG 4.11). That is why different people achieve different results, although their endeavours seem similar.

> *Human eyes see only the external endeavour, but divine eyes see the mood behind the endeavour and reciprocate accordingly. This cannot be called partiality on God's part.*

Not just for God, isn't it natural for everyone? If people treat us respectfully, we give them respect and if they mistreat us, we may respond suitably.

Unlike ordinary human beings, the Lord does not discriminate between friends and foes, the favourable and the unfavourable, because for Him there is no conception of higher and lower. Nonetheless, He reciprocates with people according to the level of their consciousness. Even with His devotees, the Lord accepts the mood behind their service rather than the quantity of service. For instance, Lord Rama was equally pleased with a small squirrel who was simply bringing some grains of sand as He was with Hanuman, who was lifting heavy boulders to build the bridge to Lanka.

For the Lord, the attitude behind the service is more important than the magnitude of the service.

Unbiased and Inescapable Verdicts

By the order of a court judge, one person is imprisoned and another person may be released from jail. One who is imprisoned must have done something criminal and is being punished for that. The one who is released from jail must have displayed a positive transformation in character, and hence he is released. Both imprisonment and release are taking place by the orders of the judge. But is the judge responsible for their distress of imprisonment or happiness of release?

An unbiased judge gives an appropriate verdict that is inescapable.

Their experiences are due to their own activities and qualities. Although the judge is the ultimate authority on behalf of the government, justice is administered according to the activities of people, and the government is not responsible for their happiness or distress. An ideal government is equal to all the citizens. Similarly, God is neutral to everyone, but for the maintenance of law and order in the universe, His supreme government has various governing laws that control the experiences of various living beings as per their moods and deeds.

Everyone reaps the results of their own good or bad acts and mentalities.

The Lord is the ultimate cause of both happiness and distress of all people since He is the creator of everything, including the system of *karma*. But He is impartial in awarding the results of our activities, whether pleasant or unpleasant. Considering all the above examples, one cannot attribute partiality to the Lord, the Supreme Father who naturally loves everyone.

Our Approach Matters

A cup of milk can be perceived by different people in different ways. One can come in contact with the milk through any of the five senses—eyes, ears, nose, skin and tongue. One who just sees the milk understands it as some white substance. One who just hears about the milk will only know some information about its characteristics, nutrient values and so on. One who just smells the milk might only relish its aroma. And one who just touches the milk might feel that it is a hot or cold liquid. But one who drinks the milk gets the real advantage of the milk by satisfying his hunger and getting nourished. The substance—milk—is same in all the five cases. But one derives the maximum advantage of milk by drinking it rather than just seeing, touching, smelling or hearing about it. Here, milk is not partial, but different people experienced it according to their approach. If this is true of milk, it is even more so when we speak of God. The Lord reciprocates according to the way we approach Him.

Mature spiritualists understand the Lord's impartial nature and see both distress and happiness as sanctioned

by the Lord in response to their own past deeds. They are convinced that the Lord has made such an arrangement to rectify their mistakes and uplift their consciousness.

A Sneak Peek into God's [Im]partiality

Once, before the Kurukshetra war, Duryodhana went to Lord Krishna's palace to ask for His assistance in the war. Arjuna also arrived for the same purpose a little while after Duryodhana. At that time, Lord Krishna was asleep. Duryodhana marched straight to the head of Lord Krishna's bed and sat there, but Arjuna stood at Lord Krishna's feet, with his palms folded as he gazed at Lord Krishna's face with utmost love.

After a while, Lord Krishna woke up. As He opened His eyes, He saw Arjuna. Lord Krishna then sat up and saw Duryodhana by His head. He welcomed both and inquired the purpose of their visit.

Duryodhana said, 'I have come here to seek Your assistance in the war. I came before Arjuna. So, it is only right that You assist me rather than him.' Lord Krishna smiled and said, 'I agree that *you arrived* first, but I *saw* Arjuna first! Further, the scriptures ordain that one should help the youngest first, so I will allow Arjuna to put His request first.'

Duryodhana became somewhat upset upon seeing Lord Krishna's partiality.

Lord Krishna then said, 'I have an army of one million soldiers called the Narayani-sena, all equal to Me in battle. One of you may take them and the other may take Me

alone. But I will not fight! I shall leave My weapons aside during the entire battle. O Arjuna, what do you choose?'

Hearing this, Duryodhana became anxious of what Arjuna would choose—an invincible army or an unarmed Lord Krishna? To his surprise, Arjuna chose Lord Krishna without a moment's hesitation.

Duryodhana's joy knew no bounds, and he could hardly conceal it. He thought, 'Arjuna's sentimentality had overpowered his reason. He had forsaken a powerful army and preferred Lord Krishna, who would not even fight. What foolishness!'

Smiling mildly, Duryodhana said, 'It seems then that I am left with the army. I shall accept it.' He took permission from Lord Krishna and departed.

Evil Duryodhana neither loved Lord Krishna nor trusted Him, while Arjuna was just the opposite. Lord Krishna showcased the qualities of Arjuna and Duryodhana by apparently being partial to Arjuna, as a natural reciprocation of his devotion.

Does God Hate Bad People?

No! God hates no one. God disapproves the nefarious activities of demoniac people, but He never disowns them.

Sometimes people question, 'Why does the Lord permit sinful activities?' The answer is that the Lord does not want anyone to act sinfully. He begs them through their good conscience to refrain from sin. But when someone insists upon acting sinfully, He sanctions it at their own risk.

The Lord tries to rectify the mentality of wrongdoers, and He is willing to forgive their misdeeds, but He doesn't interfere with their free will or independence.

Lord Krishna supported the Pandavas in the Battle of Kurukshetra against the evil Duryodhana and company. It was He who encouraged Bhima to break the thighs of Duryodhana during the fight. But at the end of battle, when Duryodhana lay on the ground with his thighs broken, Lord Krishna was not happy to see him so.

The Lord is obliged to punish a wrongdoer, but He is not happy to do so, because all living entities are originally His children.

Lord Krishna attempted to give good counsel to Duryodhana and rectify his vile mentality; unfortunately, Lord Krishna's advice only fell on deaf ears. Furthermore, Duryodhana readily accepted the polluted advice of his wicked companions—Shakuni, Dushasana and Karna. A wrongdoer is thus misled by bad associates and acts against the laws of God. He thus becomes an object of God's punishment. This is not God's partiality.

But if one obeys the principles laid down by the Lord through the scriptures, one surely travels on the path of eternal happiness. The Lord is harder than the thunderbolt for the wrongdoer and softer than the rose petals for the faithful. Similarly, when the king of demons, Ravana, kidnapped Mother Sita by coming in the disguise of a mendicant, Lord Ramachandra gave him several

opportunities to return Sita and save his life, but Ravana was so stubborn that, ultimately, Rama had to kill him.

> *God wants to rectify the mentality of miscreants, but when they become too adamant, He punishes or kills them, not out of revenge, but to liberate them from their evil mentality.*

A New Dimension to Equality

When a young boy is well-behaved, his mother appreciates or embraces him. But when he does mischief, his mother chastises him. Both acts are expressions of her love, although one appears pleasant and the other harsh. The mother's dealing with the child is attuned to the child's mood and deeds, but her underlying emotion is love. The same holds true for God.

When God is strict with some people and punishes them, that is only out of His compassion for them. When He kills a demon, He liberates him from his demoniac life. Thus, the Lord is the well-wisher of everyone and He shows compassion to different people in different ways, according to their condition. Though apparently Lord Krishna punishes or kills the demons, He looks for reasons to show them His causeless mercy and liberates them.

> *The Lord's causeless mercy in liberating both the devotees and the demons clearly distinguishes Him from ordinary living entities.*

Although the Lord is 'partial' to His devotees, He is not inimical to the miscreants. He is equal and 'impartial' to everyone, because He gives an opportunity to everyone to become His devotee, so that He can become 'partial' to them. Lord Krishna gives similar opportunities to everyone to perform *bhakti-yoga* and become His devotee just like Arjuna.

In fact, He implores everyone to become His devotee (BG 18.65). This teaching of the Bhagavad-Gita is not just for Arjuna, but for everyone. Lord Krishna promises that if one becomes His devotee, one will surely enter the eternal and joyful spiritual abode. Thus, Lord Krishna invites everyone into His loving company, equally and impartially.

> *Lord Krishna is not just partial to His devotees, but He is impartially partial to all living beings in giving them an opportunity to perform bhakti and come to His eternal abode to be with Him forever.*

Practices for Inner Balance

1. *Avoid Partiality:* Avoid favouritism, knowing well that whether it is in the family, education or ordinary transactions, partiality can lead to disappointment, demotivation and even rebellion.
2. *Understand Justifiability:* Before questioning why some suffer while others prosper, try to appreciate the existence of a divine management of the experiences of individuals according to their virtue and vice.
3. *Appreciate Divine Reciprocation:* While God is equal to all, He reciprocates according to individuals' virtues and mindsets. This is not partiality but a natural response to different approaches.
4. *Appreciate Attitude over Magnitude:* Embrace the idea that, unlike ordinary human interactions, the Lord values the attitude behind service more than the quantity of service. Understand that even small acts with a genuine and positive attitude are pleasing to the Divine.
5. *Accept Responsibility:* Understand that experiences of happiness or distress are the results of individuals' actions and qualities, as orchestrated by the Lord who is like an unbiased judge. Accept responsibility for your actions.

20

Did God Create the Bad in This World?

Practical Perspectives on God's Relationship with Evil

One day, as I stood on the ashram terrace, I was absorbed in marvelling at the rising sun at daybreak. The splendour of the morning sun was truly a sight to behold. The reddish sun had awoken and had risen from the lap of the mountains. Piercing through the puffy clouds was its warm light that soothed me. I stood there, dazed, waiting to offer a 'good morning' to this beautiful bright circle. The birdsong and cool breeze simply enhanced the pleasure of the moment. Minutes passed and soon I realized it was time for me to head back to the ashram. Turning around, I bumped into my own shadow—a sight that contrasted with the experience that I just had.

Suddenly, a thought struck me. 'Who created this dark shadow? If the sun weren't there behind me, I wouldn't see the shadow before me,' I thought. It was

the sun—the source of bright light—that caused the dark shadow to fall ahead of me. I had found an answer to my investigation.

It was at that moment that my mind suddenly transported me to the pages of the Gita (10.8) where we find Lord Krishna saying, '*aham sarvasya prabhavo*—I am the source of everything.'

Now, you may ask, 'If the Lord is the source of everything, is He the source of the bad in this world too? Can't God create only good without bad? Why does the sun that emanates light also cast a shadow? Can't the sun create only bright light without dark shadows?'

The questions are valid. But before we discuss them further, please consider this example: Imagine a man goes on a murderous rampage at a marketplace. In response to these heinous acts, the government decides to impose a death sentence. Is the government the cause of his suffering? I am sure you agree that he invited it upon himself. Blaming the government would be unjust. The man's actions forced the government to respond with punitive measures. This scenario draws parallels to the relationship with God. God doesn't create suffering; it is we who invite suffering upon ourselves. God merely sanctions our suffering, in response to our misdeeds.

Perception and Perspective

Now, if you recall, when did I exactly see the bright sunlight?
'When I faced the sun!'

And when did I see the dark shadow? 'When I turned my back towards the sun.'

Similarly, when I turn towards the teachings of God in the Gita and other wisdom texts, I experience only good in this world. But when I think whimsically and act against His divine teachings, I encounter the dark side of this world. And I believe this is true for both me and you.

Darkness is nothing but the absence of light. If we remain in light, we need not experience darkness and get scared or insecure. Similarly, bad is simply the absence of good. If all of us individually and collectively stick to good virtues, we need not witness bad.

Envy, malice, jealousy, greed, pride and other such vices exist in this world only to the point humanity slackens its march towards cultivating positive qualities like compassion, kindness, gratefulness, truthfulness and so on.

If we see the good and bad in this world from this perspective, then we wouldn't possibly raise a question like, 'Why isn't God doing anything about the bad in this world?'

The Lord doesn't deliberately create, sanction or endorse the vice in this world. In fact, He loves to see everyone virtuous and exemplary in their thoughts, words and actions. Whenever we wholeheartedly try and pray to give up vice and embrace virtue, we are sure to find the Lord extending His hand of support. And if you're confused about what you could include in your

prayer to God, here's a Vedic one from the Bṛhadāraṇyaka Upaniṣad for you:

> *'asato mā sadgamaya'—Please lead me from falsehood (evil) to the truth (good)*
>
> *'tamaso mā jyotirgamaya'—Please lead me from darkness (ignorance) to light (knowledge)*
>
> *'mṛtyormā'mṛtam gamaya'—Please lead me from death to immortality*

If we follow the noble teachings of the holy texts like the Bhagavad-Gita, we will see our lives fill up with goodness. Conversely, if we act impulsively, we may experience negativity. Individually and collectively, if we turn towards the Supreme Lord's divine teachings, coming through any of His bona fide representatives, and live a life in accordance with those teachings and values, then we will have goodness, happiness, satisfaction, serenity and sanity in this world as well as in our interactions and relationships. But if we turn our faces away from the Lord, we turn our faces towards distress.

Intensity and Intention

To the degree we seek the Lord's shelter by embracing the path of devotion or *bhakti-yoga*—the essence of the Bhagavad-Gita, and to the extent we are sincere in our spiritual practices and in cultivating noble virtues, to that degree we remain aloof from the negativity of the world. Now that's what I call spiritual mathematics.

As the sun rises early in the morning, its tepid light creates large shadows behind us. As the sun ascends in the sky, our shadows become smaller. And by midday, when the sun shines right above our heads, our shadows nearly fade away. Similarly, when the intensity of our devotion to the Lord and spiritual practice is strong, we become oblivious to the sorrows of life, barely even noticing them. However, when the intensity of our *bhakti* or absorption in spiritual practices is weak, the tribulations and temptations of this world impact us.

Oftentimes, people take to spirituality and perform some rituals, chant some *mantras* and participate in sacrifices and so on. All of this mostly to relieve themselves from suffering and gain material prosperity. But I have seen sincere spiritualists worship God with pure and selfless intentions, free of the desire for material returns. I have heard from many sincere spiritualists how they experienced the Lord reciprocate with them.

We transcend bad and experience good in life depending on the intention and intensity of our spiritual practices.

You may ask: 'Yes, it is clear that the good and bad in this world depend on our perception and perspective, and we are affected by the good and bad depending on the intensity and intention of our spiritual practices. But can't the all-powerful Lord purify everyone's intentions and make all of us do only good and thus avoid all bad actions and reactions completely?'

Well, let's find out together.

Can't God Make Everyone Good?

If even ordinary hypnotists in this world can make people do what they want them to do, then why can't the all-powerful God make everyone good? The truth is, if God desires, He can, within a moment, make all of us righteous and destroy all the bad in this world, thus establishing only good. He can enable everyone to follow His teachings exclusively and prevent us from deviating from the path of *bhakti*.

But He will not do so! And why is that?

Consider a situation where you feel thirsty and ask for water. If someone brings you water out of concern and offers it lovingly, you'd be happy and grateful. But if someone is forced to bring you water, without personal inspiration or love, and they don't offer it willingly, would you be comfortable drinking that water even if you're thirsty? You might have the water if you're desperate, but it wouldn't be a comfortable experience. Just as we aren't comfortable accepting forced love and service, we can't expect God to accept forced love, service or followership.

The Lord is supremely independent, and as His fragmental parts, we also have some independence. He never interferes with our minute independence or autonomy, even though He's capable of doing so. He sanctions the amount of free will we deserve based on our previous actions and doesn't interfere with it. If He were to program us in a way that we act according to His will, we would be no better than machines.

Interference with Independence

The Lord doesn't want to interfere with our minute independence and forcefully make us do good or be good.

He wants us to voluntarily adopt spiritual practices, service and good behaviour. He certainly tries to inspire us to become good and gives us the knowledge about the consequences of good and bad activities, but He doesn't force or hypnotize us into doing what He desires. If someone thinks of doing something immoral, the Lord begs them through their conscience, the inner voice, not to do so. But if the person is still adamant in doing so, the Lord allows them to do it at their own risk.

If we misuse our God-given independence, we end up doing bad things and experience bad results. On the other hand, if we consciously cultivate good qualities through the appropriate use of our independence, we guarantee ourselves goodness.

At any point, we have a choice to act good or bad, but we have no choice in the consequences of those acts.

Whether it's good or bad, happiness or distress, success or failure, every reality is ultimately created and sanctioned by the Lord, in the sense that He has sanctioned a certain amount of independence to every living being. However, the existence of bad is a result of the carnal desires of living beings and not the desire of the Lord. If the ability to desire is taken away from a living being, then there is no

meaning in calling people 'living beings', for they would be no better than programmed robots.

Ignorance is not the cause of every mistake that we make. We commit wrong actions even knowingly. It is our attachment to the 'pleasure' in the activity that makes us pay no heed to the good advice to avoid it. How then can we expect to avoid the consequences?

Doesn't a chain smoker know that 'cigarette smoking is injurious to health'? Isn't an alcoholic aware that alcohol consumption causes disease? If they consciously choose to smoke or drink and end up ruining their lives, how is God to be blamed?

When someone's desires, aspirations and fantasies cross the boundaries of morality, one inevitably engages in animalistic and demonic deeds which may even trouble other living beings around them. For instance, if one's lust crosses boundaries and induces infidelity, one gets into illicit connections and may even exploit the innocent in unmentionable ways. If the urges of the tongue and the belly step over the fence, one mercilessly kills innocent animals and munches on their flesh. Similarly, a money-monger may indulge in scams and scandals and even shamelessly plunder the money of the innocent. There is no end to committing such obnoxious acts, which are the result of a deficiency of goodness. Lord Krishna elaborately explains in the sixteenth chapter of Bhagavad-Gita the nightmarish consequences of such activities—like entering hellish existence, suffering for several lifetimes and so on. Therefore, the solution lies in *consciously* choosing good and abstaining from bad.

God's Attempts to Eliminate Bad

The all-merciful Lord patiently waits for us to develop virtues and devotion. Although He doesn't interfere with our minute independence, He doesn't leave us to rot in the material world, experiencing inevitable miseries. He inspires us to come to Him in the spiritual world, the ultimate destination for eternal spiritual happiness. Whenever the nefarious activities of people in this world break all boundaries, He personally descends on this planet and establishes virtue, as He declares in this popular verse in the Gita.

yadā yadā hi dharmasya
glānir bhavati bhārata
abhyutthānam adharmasya
tadātmānam sṛjāmy aham

Lord Krishna says, 'Whenever and wherever there is a decline in *dharma* or virtue and increase of *adharma* or vice, I descend on this planet, to reverse the situation' (BG 4.7).

In the next verse, Lord Krishna reveals the purposes of His various incarnations (*avatāras*), namely protecting the virtuous, punishing the vicious and establishing righteousness. Not only does He personally descend as incarnations, He also makes holy scriptures like the Gita and the Puranas available to educate and inspire us to come to the spiritual path. He sends forth His empowered representatives—the spiritual gurus—who share the divine teachings with every living entity. In this way, the Lord inspires us to voluntarily choose good and relinquish

bad. Still, the Lord leaves the decision to us to make the right choice.

The Choice Is Ours!

> *The autonomy to go on the right or the wrong path always lies with the individuals, who are responsible for their good or bad experiences in life because they are the consequences of their own choices.*

In this world, many people are not comfortable thinking of themselves as subordinate to anyone, including God. But it is in our best interest to accept the shelter of God and His representatives at various levels. Submissiveness to Almighty God and the authorized spiritual gurus who are God's transparent representatives constitutes one of the vital aspects of human life.

This eliminates the chaos caused by badness and enables us to embrace the calm of good qualities in this world. When we individually and collectively make that conscious choice, we find ourselves in the shelter of calm, far away from the reach of chaos.

Practices for Inner Balance

1. *Positive Perception and Perspective*: View challenges as opportunities for growth, shaping your experience through a positive lens. Cultivate virtues such as compassion and avoid negativity.
2. *Spiritual Intensity and Intent*: Approach spiritual practices and devotion with sincerity and intensity. Understand that the depth of your connection and intention shields you from negativity.
3. *Consciously Choose Good*: Acknowledge your autonomy in decision-making and personal responsibility in shaping experiences. Make conscious choices aligned with virtues, avoiding actions driven by negative desires.
4. *Seek God's Shelter and Spiritual Guidance*: Embrace humility and learn from spiritual gurus and authentic representatives, actively pursuing a spiritual path aligned with goodness for personal calm and collective harmony.
5. *Personal Responsibility in the Face of Suffering*: Much like a government responding to actions, God doesn't cause our suffering; our choices decide if we should be happy or suffer. Our actions influence our experiences

21

The Leadership Riddle

Modern Dilemmas in Mentorship and Micromanagement

Long ago, I saw a mother making her little baby walk next to her by holding his hand. For a moment, I thought, 'Why can't she just pick up the baby and carry him in her arms? After all, the child is so small, unable to walk and doesn't seem too heavy to carry!' The baby looked cute. Any onlooker would be excited to take the child in their hands or lap, play and relish his sweet smiles—so, why is the mother acting in this way?

Thereafter, I made a thoughtful observation and reflection, after which I could understand and appreciate her dealing with her baby in that way. In fact, we can learn a lot of life lessons on mentorship by analysing how mothers train their children in walking. Trust me, I'm not giving you tall tales.

When the child is just a couple of months old, a mother consciously makes her child walk. Initially, she keeps the

child's feet on hers and holds the child's hands with her own. Then she slowly begins to walk backward to teach the child to move forward.

After a while, she stops offering her feet as support and allows the child to walk on the floor while she holds his hands. With time, she offers only one hand. As time progresses, she simply offers a finger.

After some time, the mother totally desists from offering any kind of support. She would probably sit on a chair and call out to her child or even gesticulate only, so that her child can take the first step of independence. Multiple times at this stage, I have seen a mother's emotions flow out of her mouth as she verbally nudges her toddler saying, 'Come, come to me.' The child may walk a few steps, fall on his bottom, but the mother doesn't come to pick up the kid. Sitting or standing at a distance, she keeps encouraging the child to get up and walk towards her.

This generally uplifts the child's spirit, and in no time, the baby is back up on his little feet and waddles his way to his mother. In the end, they enter a loving embrace with their faces breaking into beautiful smiles. And this, my friends, is what we technically call 'training'.

All mothers have the ability, love and attachment to keep their little kids on their lap or lend a hand to them all the time, but practically, they don't do so. Because this would prevent the child from learning to walk.

Trainers in various fields should probably learn from mothers on how to train juniors.

Someday, the child has to outgrow the mother's lap. Spoon-feeding has its limits. The child cannot and should not be spoon-fed for a long time but must be allowed to grow up self-sufficiently, stand on his own legs and do his own work.

Now, join me on an exploration of the dynamics of mentorship. What's more, we'll have direct guidance from Lord Krishna's dealings with Arjuna in the Gita. A quick note before we start off—the term 'mentor–mentee relationship' is a broad term and encapsulates the parent–child, teacher–student, senior–junior, boss–assistant, employer–employee and guardian–dependant relationship.

I Need a Mentor—Seriously!?

While everyone craves independence, not everyone possesses the maturity to wield this independence constructively. In such cases, guidance and corrections coming in from an experienced person often prove beneficial. Everyone needs mentors in life. No one is born wise.

Mentors aren't an obstruction on our way to independence. They are the map.

Within the purview of the role of a mentor is their corrective intervention in the lives of their mentees. A wise man called Chanakya Pandit once said:

lālane bahavo doṣās
tāḍane bahavo guṇāh
tasmāt putram ca śiṣyam ca
tāḍayen na tu lālayet

'Pampering a subordinate will increase his faults. Chastising him will increase his good qualities. So, rather than pamper unduly, a teacher must chastise a student, and a father must chastise a child.'

Lord Krishna, too, highlights this principle. Before the battle at Kurukshetra, Lord Krishna chastised a disinclined Arjuna saying, 'This kind of mentality doesn't befit a *kshatriya* like yourself. It leads to infamy. Give up such petty weakness of heart and fight' (BG 2.2-3).

In my life, I've had multiple mentors and I feel the strength of their contribution even today. I distinctly remember the umpteen corrections they put me through. But in the end, I was a better man. Their sensibility worked wonders. I remember them employing various set-ups—feedback, counteractions and cautions—they would deploy the best and most suitable strategy. But they were far from simply being mentors. They loved me as their son and this was what their treatment spoke. That's when I learnt that being a mentor isn't about being a dominating, grumpy fault-finder. It's about genuinely caring for your trainees.

> *Mentorship is a selfless service, and not an opportunity for self-aggrandizement or a means to exercise control over others.*

Goodbye to Dear Mentor

During childhood, one's dependence on one's parents is greater, but as one grows, the need to develop into a self-sufficient version of oneself increases. What if our

parents were still required to do our shoelaces or pack our bag to work?

Here's another pertinent statement from Chanakya Pandit: 'Indulge a son until he is five years old, and then discipline him for another ten years. When he has attained the sixteenth year, treat him as a friend.'

When a student is young, the teacher may wish to encourage him by tolerating innocent mistakes and, if required, correct lovingly. But when the student is a little older and has developed a relationship with the teacher, the latter may frankly and strictly correct mistakes. With the passage of time, as a student becomes more experienced, a teacher will put in much less effort supervising him and treat him like a friend. Similarly, a mentor may occasionally give suggestions when required to a grown-up mentee, while acknowledging the mentee's good work, experience and status.

Correction that intimidates a junior and makes the senior unapproachable is unhealthy for the relationship.

Everyone needs guidance, but not in everything and not at all times. A mentor is not someone who constantly chases mentees and intervenes to adjust their decisions and actions. Mentors should not micromanage, spoon-feed or unduly criticize the youngsters but give them training, advice, knowledge and reasonable freedom to make certain decisions appropriate to their age and experience. A mentor respects the choices and opinions of grown-up mentees, unless they are absurd.

Acknowledging Autonomy

God is supremely autonomous. As a fragmental part (*amsha*) of God, every living being also has autonomy, but to a minute degree. God doesn't interfere with the autonomy of the living entity, although He is able to do so. Similarly, mature mentors, teachers and parents also shouldn't overly interfere with the autonomy of those whom they guide.

Lord Krishna did the same with Arjuna on the battlefield of Kurukshetra. When Arjuna was confused, Lord Krishna explained the Bhagavad-Gita, and at the end, He said, '*vimṛśyaitad aśeṣeṇa yathecchasi tathā kuru*—Deliberate on what I have explained to you fully, and then do what you wish to do' (BG 18.63). These concluding words indicate that God does not interfere with our little independence. He doesn't force anyone to act according to His instructions but gives knowledge and then allows people to act as per their choice and understanding.

> *Mature mentors don't micromanage or spoon-feed their mentees. Instead of imposing their opinions, they inspire by personal example.*

A father can easily give his child the answer to a simple maths problem, but unless he restrains himself from doing so, the child may not learn arithmetic. Older children, especially, may be awkward when mothers overly instruct them in doing even trivial things. Micromanaging someone's activities can dishearten and demotivate them, impeding their creativity and organic growth. Corrective

actions can sometimes turn out to be dreadful, such as when they diminish the inspiration and enthusiasm of a subordinate. Guides should allow people to grow organically by learning from mistakes.

Too much help from an elder can limit the independent thinking of a learner.

A mentor is not meant to demotivate or discourage mentees through undue intrusions into their freedom but inspire and assist them to grow into mature individuals. A senior cannot always expect a junior to agree to instructions, especially when the senior is exercising authority arbitrarily. The mentor should be willing to hear the mentee's thoughts, opinions and preferences. And if the mentee, for a genuine reason, is unable to accede to the instruction, the mentor should be willing to accommodate, without getting offended or feeling undervalued.

Mentors' value is not just in how much their instructions are being followed, but in how much they are valuing the people whom they mentor.

The 24-Karat Mentor

Sometimes, while acting as mentors, we tend to impose our ideologies and expectations on others. Can you recall a time when this happened with you or you have done so to someone?

Maybe it was truly our need to guide them more than their need to receive guidance. And that's how we depend

on others' dependence on us. Rather than being a source of inspiration to others, we sometimes end up instigating them to fulfil our dreams, wishing to see our desires and expectations manifest through them!

Forced mentorship either in day-to-day life or in spirituality intimidates and discomforts people. Unsolicited suggestions and feedback, especially when presented in a forceful manner, can have unpleasant outcomes. Also, it's important to note that no matter how great a piece of advice may be, if the receiver is not receptive, its value is not revealed.

Guidance shouldn't intimidate or impose upon people but inspire them.

We need to make sure we don't mentor people out of a desire to control. I have personally observed how the most inconvincible people accept and practise a piece of advice when their independence is not encroached upon. And the opposite is true when they are counselled more coercively.

True mentorship is never about collecting name and fame. It's about making sure our mentee is on the path to growth.

Sometimes, we also see people posing as mentors on subjects whose names they can't spell. And I think this is truly dangerous for the mentor–mentee relationship. My beloved spiritual Guru once said, 'It is violence to give guidance without experience.' The word 'experience' must be understood deeply. Experience comes not only by undergoing something personally but also by carefully

observing situations and people, rationally analysing the situation at hand and learning lessons from it. If we see someone being arrested on the grounds of thievery, we must understand that stealing is bad, without actually stealing and getting arrested!

Tightrope Walk—Drawing Balance

Not intruding into autonomy doesn't mean remaining quiet despite witnessing a younger one's struggles, by restricting oneself from sharing wisdom. As mentors, we shouldn't restrict others' freedom of choice, but at the same time, we should protect them from acting whimsically in the name of freedom.

When it is evident that the person is struggling and we have the capacity to help, we must not hesitate to offer a helping hand. It could be correction, feedback, suggestions or some ruffling words in accordance with the circumstances.

A wise and compassionate person is called *para dukha dukhi*—one who feels distressed seeing others' distress. When surgery is unavoidable, a surgeon shouldn't hesitate to pierce the patient's body with knives and scissors, but only after a dose of anaesthesia!

Be a Well-Wisher and Empower

A critical quality of a mentor is to be a genuine well-wisher. Genuine concern builds trust and acceptance beyond being seen as a source of knowledge. Responsible mentorship doesn't force suggestions but proactively

offers solutions with love and relatability. True mentors empower mentees to make better decisions, elevating consciousness.

Good mentors are realistic, not idealistic. They do not suppress the individuality of mentees but empower them to think on their own.

When Lord Krishna asked Arjuna to choose his plan of action after having heard the Gita, Arjuna stood silently ruminating on the very deep meaning of the Gita. Glancing at His dear friend, Lord Krishna's merciful heart melted like butter and He spoke, 'Dear friend, I will now speak the essence of the whole scripture in a few verses. Forget about the difficulties in having to review everything to understand it.'

Then Lord Krishna concluded saying, 'Again, hear My divine advice, the most confidential knowledge of all. I speak this for your benefit, because you are My very dear friend, and have faith in Me. Always think of Me, become My devotee, worship Me and offer obeisances unto Me. By this, you will attain supreme peace (*param santim*) and My personal abode in the spiritual world. Give up all varieties of religion, and just surrender unto Me alone. I shall deliver you from all sinful reactions. Do not worry' (BG 18.64–66).

This personal reassurance of Lord Krishna made Arjuna even more attracted to Lord Krishna's love. At the end of the Gita, Arjuna was not only convinced of his duty as a warrior but also of Lord Krishna's affection

and well-wishing intent, and happily agreed to follow his advice with full commitment.

> *When there is a well-wishing intent, people automatically trust us and rely on a mentor's guidance.*
>
> *Healthy mentorship involves care, concern and compassion, while unhealthy mentorship relies on force and imposition.*

When I Am a Mentee . . .

Being a mentee doesn't mean suppressing our intelligence and individuality in the name of submissiveness. Instead, we can harmonize both, just like Arjuna.

Arjuna was both faithful and thoughtful in accepting Lord Krishna's instructions. Blind faith without intelligence or intelligence without good faith is neither prescribed nor appreciated. A thoughtful and faithful balance in the mentor–mentee relationship fosters fruitful outcomes.

Being obedient to a respectable senior like a parent, a eacher or an elder is a fundamental human virtue. This is ecommended and appreciated in all cultured societies. For nstance, Lord Rama and Lord Krishna were submissive to Their parents and teachers, and served them respectfully ven if their instructions were sometimes difficult o follow.

> *God, while playing the role of a human being in this world, sets an example for the entire humanity to follow.*

The pleasure of our parents, teachers and honourable elders with our moods and deeds acts as a great blessing upon us and empowers us to accomplish even difficult things. We need to be grateful for all the guidance, support, blessings and favours received from our guides, and in reciprocation for their support, we need to serve to the best of our ability, with all sincerity.

The gold that isn't smelted in fire doesn't shine. So does a person who undergoes no refinement under the guidance of an expert guide. Similarly, a person who doesn't undergo the necessary training from an experienced mentor doesn't grow to his full potential.

Whether one is a student at school or a trainee at the military camp, one should be open to feedback and correction solely for one's own improvement. One must trust the intentions and integrity of a reliable guide whose treatment might sometimes appear harsh and strict.

Intelligent and sensible subordinates are not offended by a superior's suggestions. They are grateful to receive instructions for improvement. They are not unduly attached to their autonomy. Such humble subordinates make the best of their superior's experience and wisdom becoming close to their hearts. Submissive and simple subordinates, through their loyalty to their superiors become accomplished in their endeavours. They win trust and are empowered with more knowledge, responsibility and opportunities to excel.

When the mature mentor doesn't feel confident about a mentee's reception of a correction, the mentee loses an opportunity to grow.

Brittle subordinates who are possessive and independent and don't invite any intrusions into their autonomy, even by their experienced seniors, have little possibility to flourish. On the other hand, malleability makes a subordinate praiseworthy. That requires sacrifice, obedience and the willingness to extend oneself despite inconveniences.

Submissiveness to the Lord, the gurus and their transparent representatives constitutes one of the vital aspects of spiritual advancement.

A Meaningful Mentor–Mentee Relationship

Sensible seniors respect the autonomy of grown-up juniors and allow them to grow, without micromanaging or spoon-feeding them. They tolerate honest mistakes and if necessary, gently correct their juniors, giving due credit for good work performed. On the other hand, sensible juniors are willing to be corrected by experienced seniors without getting offended. They feel fortunate to be guided and invite intrusions into their autonomy that help them improve and render better service. When such sensibleness is maintained by both superiors and subordinates—whether teacher and student, master and servant, employer and employee, or God and devotee—their relationship becomes sweet and their interactions, free of tension and insecurity, become nourishing.

A mentor who sensitively respects the autonomy of a mentee, and a mentee who sensibly uses their autonomy while respecting the mentor, make an exemplary mentor-mentee relationship.

It really won't be difficult for us to spot the encouragement, support and affection a true mentor gives his mentees. Also, looking for qualities like respectfulness, gratefulness and submissiveness in a true mentee is no needle-in-a-haystack task. Thus, when one lacks such an understanding, one maintains an immature attitude in their mentor–mentee relationship, thus ruining what could have been a life-changing experience.

Practices for Inner Balance

1. *Progressive Guidance*: While mentoring people, be dynamic by beginning with comprehensive support and gradually reduce guidance as the mentee evolves by experience.
2. *Well-wishing Intent*: Prioritize the mentee's growth over personal gain or control. Genuinely care for their well-being, as a selfless service aimed at empowering mentees to make better decisions.
3. *Acknowledge Autonomy*: Provide feedback with empathy but avoid domination and micromanagement. Inspire growth through personal example and don't force ideologies on them. Encourage open communication and empower them to make age-appropriate choices.
4. *Don't Go to Extremes*: Find a balance between respecting the mentee's autonomy and offering assistance when needed. Intervene timely and wisely to protect the mentee from whimsical actions.
5. *Make Relationships Meaningful*: Tolerate mistakes, correct gently and give due credit for good work. Foster an atmosphere where mentorship is a collaborative, nourishing experience for both parties involved.

Acknowledgements

Words fall short of expressing my gratitude to Srila Prabhupada, the founder Acharya of the International Society for Krishna Consciousness, who presented the divine literature Bhagavad-Gita with his lucid explanations. It is through the lens of his illuminating purports that I have learnt to understand the depth of the Gita.

I am forever indebted to my beloved Guru, His Holiness Radhanath Swami, the founder of Govardhan Ecovillage and an international bestselling author, for enlightening me on the ideal mood of scriptural study and encouraging me with his kind blessings. I learnt profound truths of life by listening to his discourses and by observing his exemplary dealings. I express my earnest gratitude to my mentor Gauranga Prabhu, and many other great spiritual teachers and friends who inspired me in various ways in my spiritual journey.

I can't thank the young brothers Parth Shah and Tanay Shah enough for their dedicated efforts in proofreading and editing the manuscript, and improving the quality of the work with their wonderful suggestions and feedback.

Without the honest and selfless efforts of these two young seekers, this book wouldn't have taken such a beautiful shape.

My heartfelt gratitude to the Penguin Ananda team, including Gurveen, Anushree and Ralph for making this publication possible for the benefit of all. I sincerely thank Sagar Wadekar and Mansi Wadekar for their support and coordination.

Finally, I heartily thank all of you, the wonderful readers of this book, for taking part in relishing and reflecting on the profound insights of the Gita.

Appendix

Bhagavad-Gita Verses Quoted in the Book

Verse no.	Verse	Theme	Page no.
2.7	*kārpaṇya-doṣopahata-svabhāvah*	Finding Your Guide to Clear Confusion	60
2.13	*dehino 'smin yathā dehe*	Journey of the Eternal Soul	186
2.14	*mātrā-sparśās tu kaunteya*	The Art of Tolerance	19
2.15	*sama-duhkha-sukham dhīram*	Liberation or Relief through Equanimity	33
2.22	*vāsāmsi jīrṇāni yathā vihāya*	The Outfit of the Soul	187

2.38	*sukha-duhkhe same kṛtvā*	Equanimity and Rising above Sin	33
2.41	*vyavasāyātmikā buddhir*	Building One-Pointed Focus	87
2.47	*karmaṇy evādhikāras*	Being Actively Detached	45
2.58	*yadā samharate cāyam*	The Art of Withdrawal (a Lesson from the Tortoise)	69
2.59	*param dṛṣṭvā nivartate*	Upgrading Our Taste (Developing a Higher Purpose)	39
2.60	*yatato hy api kaunteya*	Taming the Unruly Senses	70
2.62-63	*sangāt sañjāyate kāmah*	The Anchor of Attachment	107
3.35	*śreyān sva-dharmo viguṇah*	Embracing Your Uniqueness	4
4.11	*ye yatha mam prapadyante*	God's Reciprocal Nature	225

5.18	*vidyā-vinaya-sampanne*	The Vision of the Self Realized	153
6.26	*yato yato niścalati*	The Art of Mind Control	79
6.5-6	*uddhared ātmanātmānaṁ*	Mind—Our Friend and Foe	80
7.11	*dharma aviruddho bhūteshu kāmo asmi*	Authorized Lust	109
8.15	*dukhalayam ashasvatam*	Where Pain and Transience Co-exist	217
9.14	*satatam kīrtayanto mām*	Incessant Recalling of God	169
9.29	*samo 'ham sarva-bhūteṣu*	God's Inconceivable Impartiality	223
10.8	*aham sarvasya prabhavo*	The Primal Cause behind Everything	236
10.25	*yajñānām japa-yajño 'smi*	Chanting: The Prescribed Spiritual Process	173

14.4	*aham-bija-pradah pita*	The Seed-Giving Father	223
14.5	*sattvam rajas tama iti*	Invisible Ropes That Bind All of Us	94
16.7	*yuktāhāra-vihārasya*	Neutralizing Gluttony	97
16.21	*tri-vidham narakasyedam*	Three Gates to Hell	129
17.6	*anudvega-karam vakyam, satyam priya-hitam cayat*	Influencing Hearts through Words	132
18.63	*vimṛśyaitad aśeṣeṇa yathecchasi tathā kuru*	Recommendation That Respects Autonomy	252
18.73	*naṣṭo mohah smṛtir labdhā*	Regaining our Intelligence	65